# A SHORT ARCHITECTURAL HISTORY OF WORCESTER CATHEDRAL

BY

## PHILIP BARKER
MA, FSA HonMIFA

with contributions by

KENNETH WILTSHIRE
FRIBA, FRSA
and
PROFESSOR JOHN PRENTICE
PhD, FGS, MInstGeol

FRONT COVER
The Cathedral
from Sidbury

BACK COVER
The Crypt
(Photograph by Helen Lubin)

This book is dedicated to the memory
of Charles Davidson who enthusiastically
supported the work of restoration of the Cathedral.

ISBN  0 9516274 2 2     A Short Architectural History
                        of Worcester Cathedral

PUBLISHED ON BEHALF OF THE DEAN AND
CHAPTER OF WORCESTER BY
PHILIP BARKER
4 ST. GEORGE'S SQUARE, WORCESTER, WR1 1HX

Printed By NORTHWICK PRINT VITESSE WORCESTER

# A SHORT ARCHITECTURAL HISTORY OF WORCESTER CATHEDRAL

## Contents:

# INTRODUCTION

This book has been badly needed for a long time. Worcester Cathedral is a complex building whose history reveals an organic evolution throughout the centuries. People need help to understand it and the more they understand the more they will appreciate it.

While the book has been needed for some time it is good that we have waited. Philip Barker, our Consultant Archaeologist, knows the building better than most and has drawn together the work of many previous writers, particularly that of Robert Willis, who, though writing more than 130 years ago, has hardly been superseded. The current restoration work has enabled us to learn a great deal more about the building, but there will always be further discoveries to be made and understood. This book gives us a lot of detail and is an excellent basis for further work, and it is to be hoped that it will initiate an on-going series on many different aspects of the Cathedral.

We are deeply grateful to Mrs Jean Davidson and the Friends of Worcester Cathedral who by their financial contributions have made this publication possible. Mrs Davidson made her donation in memory of her husband, Charles Davidson, who was fascinated by the Cathedral and was a great friend of ours.

I hope it will enable all readers to treasure the heritage into which we have entered.

Robert Jeffery
Dean

Worcester
January 1994

# A SHORT ARCHITECTURAL HISTORY OF WORCESTER CATHEDRAL

## Preface

There is no short, easily accessible account of the architectural development of Worcester Cathedral. This book attempts to fill that gap, but in order to make it concise and readable, it has been necessary to simplify drastically a large and complex building, to resist dwelling on detailed discussion, and sometimes to side-step controversial questions of date or influence.

Worcester's site has been continuously occupied since at least late prehistoric times, and archaeology, topography and documentary history are beginning to make clear the outlines of the development of the city from the earliest times to the present day. Nevertheless, the architectural evolution of Worcester's principal church is known only from the Norman Conquest onwards - the histories of the churches which preceded St Wulfstan's new church of 1084 are known only in barest outline, and their architectural development - even their sites - are quite unknown.

Since it is unlikely that documents relating to the pre-Norman churches remain to be discovered, further research into the early churches' sites and structures will principally be archaeological, using mainly geophysical survey and excavation. Geophysical surveys, being non-destructive, must be the first option, though they have limitations which are not yet understood. Meanwhile every opportunity to observe and record holes dug, for whatever cause, in and around the Cathedral must be taken in the hope that fragments of information will accumulate, like pieces of a jigsaw, to build a fuller picture of the past than we have today. While we are in the middle of a massive and expensive programme of restoration, there are no funds or time for research excavation on the scale required to solve some of the more intractable problems of the early churches and their surrounding monastic buildings, but economic and academic climates may change, and research excavations become possible in the comparatively near future. Meanwhile, the only excavations carried out are those demanded by the restoration programme or other emergencies.

It is difficult to write about a great building with a long history of additions, alterations and repairs, without using some technicalities. While these have been kept to a minimum, readers not familiar with architectural terms will find explanatory diagrams and a glossary at the end of the book.

This book attempts to distil the work of many scholars, architectural historians and archaeologists. In order to avoid the mass of references which would be necessary to justify every statement or opinion, these also are kept to the minimum, but lists of books containing supporting evidence and others for further reading will be found at the end of the book.

# 1. THE SITE OF THE CATHEDRAL

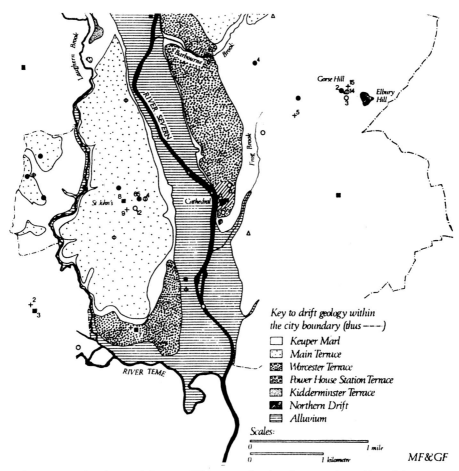

Fig 1. *Topographical map of the site of Worcester showing the strategic position of the defended core of the City at the southern tip of a ridge of sand and gravel close to a crossing point of the Severn.*
Reproduced from Barker, 1970.

Worcester is situated on the southern tip of a long ridge of sand and gravel which forms one of the terraces of the Severn laid down in post-glacial times on the edge of the river's flood plain. The suburb of St John's stands on the opposite terrace. The City occupies a promontory bounded by the Severn on the west, by the marshes of Diglis on the south and the once marshy valley of the Frog Brook on the east. The river was tidal until the construction of Diglis Weir in the 19th century, and the crossing point here would have been fordable at least twice a day, and more often when the river was low. The combination of a naturally defended site and the crossing of a major river made it an obvious choice for settlement, and Worcester's first defences probably date from the late Iron Age, that is, the last few centuries before Christ.

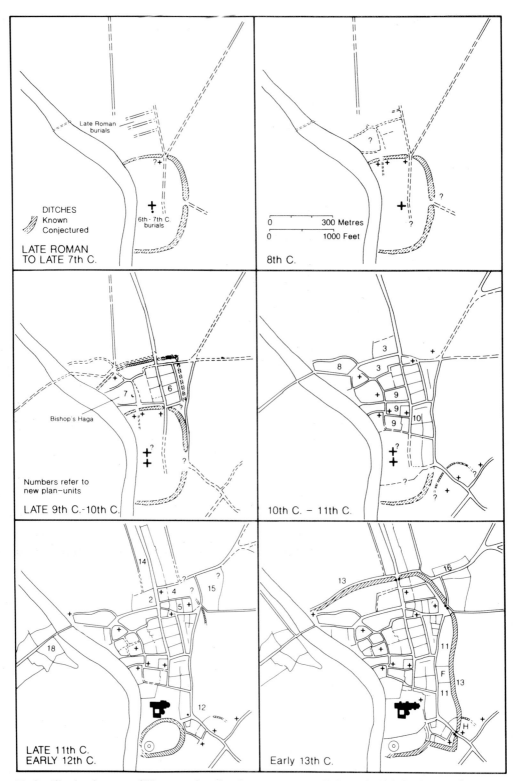

*Fig 2. The development of Worcester from late Roman times up till the early 13th C, showing the positions of the early churches and the Cathedral in relation to the defences.*

8

# 2. FROM ROMAN *VERTIS* TO NORMAN *WIRECESTRE*

Roman Worcester, whose name may have been *Vertis*, though this is not certain, occupied the same defended area as the Iron Age site, and a suburb, at first residential though later given over to iron-smelting, developed to the north. In the later Roman period the town's defences were massively enlarged on the same alignment and by this time a stone bridge may have been built a little upstream from the site of the present bridge.

Although the years between the early 5th and the late 9th centuries are obscure, there is now convincing evidence of continuity of occupation of Worcester from Roman times through to the building of the Anglo-Saxon *burh* c.880-890. This evidence derives in part from archaeology, but more from the study of the topography and the ecclesiastical history of the city.

It has been suggested that Worcester's strategic importance as a defended bridge-head on the Severn may have increased in the early post-Roman period (Bassett, 1989, 247) and that the large well-defined territory which was apparently subject to Worcester's British rulers became the parish of a church which stood in the defended enclosure. This was St Helen's. Bassett continues 'there may well be nothing Roman about St Helen's, Worcester, or about the territory around the town which became its parish, but there can be no doubt that when the first Anglo-Saxon bishop of the Hwicce arrived there, he came to a place which was already

an important Christian centre; nor that the minster founded for him was meant to take over (at least at local level) from an established British church - probably a see - serving a wide rural hinterland' (*op. cit.* 248). Two other early churches lay within the northern defences of the town - St Margaret's (now lost) and St Alban's (Baker, *et al.* 1992).

It is not clear why St Helen's, St Alban's and St Margaret's churches were all sited within the northern edge of the enclosure (fig. 2), but it has been reasonably suggested that this was because the rest of the enclosure was already occupied by buildings, perhaps dating from Roman times and still in use. While no Roman stone buildings are known from within the defended circuit, small excavations have shown that below the medieval and Anglo-Saxon occupation levels lies deep building debris including masses of roof tiles, suggesting that the Roman buildings here were of timber. Excavation in other Roman towns, for example Wroxeter in Shropshire, has shown that major buildings could be constructed of timber, so it may be that the centre of the enclosure contained Roman public buildings, or perhaps a complex of domestic buildings, all of timber. These may still have been in use in the late and sub-Roman periods, that is, the 4th to the 6th centuries AD. From the Cathedral itself the evidence for continuity of Christian worship from Roman times is significant though not conclusive. In 1973 two east-west burials of young men were found immediately under the floor of the refectory undercroft (front end paper, Z). Calibrated radio-carbon dates from the two skeletons using two standard deviations give ranges of AD 416-811 (or 852) for one skeleton, (A), and AD 449-886 for the other, (B). The see was founded in AD 680. The date for burial A therefore lies between 264 years before the foundation of the see and 172 years after it. Similarly the date for burial B lies between 231 years before the foundation of the see and 206 years after it. The balance of these dates lies therefore slightly before rather than after 680. There is, however, another factor which tilts the burial dates back towards Roman times. This is the discovery, under the neck of one of the bodies, of a tiny fragment of very fine gold braid, dated by Elizabeth Crowfoot, who examined it, to either the late Roman or the late Saxon period. As the calibrated radio-carbon dates above include the late Roman but not the late Saxon period, the balance of probability suggests that the actual dates may be before (perhaps well before) 680, the date of the foundation of the see. (Barker, *et al.* 1974 and Bassett, 1989).

The origins of the Anglo-Saxon tribe of the Hwicce, which occupied the area which eventually became the diocese of Worcester, are obscure, but they were in existence as a political unit by the early seventh century (Wilson, M in Barker *et al.* 1970). In the reorganisation of the English church, Archbishop Theodore established a see at Worcester and its first Bishop, Bosel, took office in 680.

By that time, the majority of any late Roman buildings may have fallen into disuse (the two burials under the refectory suggest that part at least of the central area had become a cemetery) leaving an open space in which Bosel could build the first Cathedral, dedicated to St Peter. We have no idea what this Cathedral was like, nor even whether it was built of timber or stone, though as it was 'still standing' in 991, and its presbytery was enlarged in stone after c.1040-41, it seems likely that it was a stone building from the first.

We do not know precisely where it was, though presumably it was within the present precinct. It has been suggested that it may have lain to the south, in the area of College Green, and been incorporated after the Conquest into the bailey of the Norman Castle, though if this were so, it is remarkable that such a loss to the monastery is not mentioned when the loss of part of the monks' cemetery to the castle bailey is recorded and deplored.

In 961 Oswald became Bishop and, as one of the leading figures in the monastic reform movement, replaced the secular priests who had served the Cathedral by a more formally organised monastic community. To house the new community he built a Cathedral dedicated to St Mary. Presumably this church was begun some time in the 960s and according to a note attached to a charter of 983, the Cathedral of St Mary was completed in that year. Another charter tells us that the church of St Peter was still standing in 991, and that the Bishop's throne was still housed in the old building.

Two writers, Hemming in the eleventh century and William of Malmesbury in the twelfth century, believed that St Mary's had been built in the cemetery of St Peter's. Hemming described Oswald, before the completion of his new church, preaching to large crowds, standing on the stone tomb of an 8th century nobleman and his wife. The tomb stood till the 1040s, when it was demolished to provide building material for the enlargement of St Peter's, mentioned above. St Peter's thus remained in use until at least the mid-eleventh century - after that nothing more is heard of it. St Mary's had a bell-tower added to it in the 1050s by Wulfstan, who was then Prior.

The Norman castle at Worcester, a timber castle of motte and bailey type, was in existence within three years of the Conquest, in 1069, when Urse d'Abitot was appointed constable. He constructed an outer bailey 'digging a ditch across the monks' burial ground'. A writer of the 18th century says "The precincts of the church were very strait or scant as it were 'pent up' between the south side of the church and the north side of the castle". However, since the monks' recovered their burial ground in 1217 it is not clear how the writer knew this in the 18th century.

In 1084, 15 years after the building of the castle, Wulstan began an entirely new and, by comparison, huge church, large parts of which still stand today, incorporated into the fabric of the present Cathedral.

## Some possible pre-Norman Walls

The west wall of the cloister, part of which was the party wall with the dormitory beyond, has, since the 19th century, been described as Anglo-Saxon, because of the large early Norman opening (now blocked) which has been cut into it (fig. 3). Another wall, west of the dormitory, and forming the east wall of the undercroft between the dormitory and the river, is also said to be Anglo-Saxon,

*Fig 3. Part of the west wall of the cloister showing the large semi-circular arched opening cut into it. This opening has the same characteristics as Wulfstan's church – a roll moulding and simple cushion capitals. The wall into which it is cut is therefore presumed to be Anglo-Saxon. The low-centred arched doorway below is of the 14th century.*

*Fig 4. A detail of the west wall of the cloister showing a blocked Norman door with at A a fragment of an earlier window. To the left, at B, is the jamb of another blocked door of uncertain date with the base of a small attached shaft at its base, C. The masonry to the right of the blocked door may be pre-Norman. The masonry blocking the Norman door appears to have been built in imitation of the pre-Norman masonry. All the cloister walls deserve very careful analysis.*

because it is made of large, heavily weathered stones, against which the 12th century vaulting of the undercroft has been built. Clearly it had been an exterior wall for a long time before the vaulting was added to it. (*Worcs. Cath. Notes* etc. 1909-1914)

There is a very similar length of wall at the extreme west end of the refectory undercroft, which, although now an internal wall, seems to have been weathered in the same way, and therefore appears also to have been external at some time.

There are two other stretches of wall in the cloister which appear to be earlier than the Norman walls which butt against them. One is the west wall of the transept between the Prior's Door and the 11th century turret in the corner of the transept which appears to have been keyed into the coursed rubble of the transept wall (fig. 5). The other is in the cloister south wall, where part of the wall, which is of course the north wall of the refectory, is also of coursed rubble, quite different from the rest of the wall and its buttresses which are of large rectangular blocks of red sandstone. Examination of the junction of the rubble wall where it meets the buttress to its east shows that the buttress is partly built against the wall and partly keyed into it. Clearly the buttress is later (fig. 6).

The common characteristics of these early rubble walls are the variety of stones used, the frequent use of diagonal joints or triangu

*Fig 5. The wall of the eastern Cloister walk between the eastern slype and the nave of the Church.*
*The coursed rubble wall appears to be earlier than the ashlar wall to the right, which is keyed into it. Since the ashlar wall is part of the 1084+ stair turret in the corner of the south transept, it follows that the rubble wall is earlier than 1084 and therefore may be Anglo-Saxon.*
*The attached shafts and springers of the cloister vault are, of course, later inserts of the 14th century.*

*Fig 6. A detail of the south wall of the cloister, i.e. the north wall of the refectory, showing a Norman buttress of massive squared ashlar with a similar wall to the left, and, to the right, a wall of roughly coursed rubble which runs behind the buttress which has been alternately keyed into it. The rubble wall is therefore earlier and very probably pre-Norman. The springing of the vault above is, of course, 14th century and can be seen to have been inserted.*
*The stove is one of the Victorian coke stoves which heated the Church.*

lar stones and, at intervals of two or three courses, thinner courses not unlike the tile courses in much Roman masonry. The western face of the western wall of the cloister (fig. 7), now an exterior face but originally the interior wall of the east end of the dormitory, shows this characteristic clearly now it has been weathered, since the lias, which forms the narrow coursing on this side, stands proud of the rest of the wall, which is of softer Highley stone. It is interesting that, though the two sides of the same wall are built of different materials, the constructional techniques are similar.

The significance of these early stretches of wall is not obvious. If they really are pre-Conquest they are presumably remains from the Anglo-Saxon monastic buildings. It is curious that they are built into three sides of the present cloister and the most obvious explanation would be that the Anglo-Saxon cloister was the same size as the present one, which seems inherently unlikely. The three sections of wall, need not, of course, have belonged to the same building, and the misalignment of the refectory with the Cathedral and the rest of the monastic buildings (see front end paper) may derive from its re-use

*Fig 7. The exterior of the west wall of the Cloister showing the blocked Perpendicular doorway into the Dormitory, D, and the blocked rectangular windows, E, above the present, late, doorway into the garden. The wall, which has thin courses of lias alternating with ?Highley stone has, since the 19th century, been thought to be Anglo-Saxon. It is unique in the Cathedral and in its construction, as is the Cloister side of the same wall (fig 4).*

of the foundations of an earlier building, of which the stretch of rubble wall in the cloister and the stretch of apparently external wall in the undercroft are all that survive above ground.

Large sections of early wall within the Cathedral are also built in somewhat similar techniques, for example, the west wall of the northern transept (fig. 9) contrasting with the adjoining stair turret.

The use of this somewhat similar walling in the early Cathedral might be explained by

the use of Anglo-Saxon masons to build lengths of wall in the manner to which they were accustomed, with Norman masons building alongside them in ashlar, for example, in the stair turrets.

All this is pure speculation, of course, but there are problems here which cannot be easily explained, and the more one examines these walls the more intractable the problems become.

# 3. ST WULFSTAN'S CATHEDRAL

St Wulfstan became Bishop in 1062 and, surviving the Norman Conquest, remained so until his death in 1095. The two Anglo-Saxon Cathedrals had been sacked by the Danes in the early 11th century and though we do not know the extent of the destruction it was certainly not total. When Wulfstan became Bishop he found only twelve monks at the monastery and he increased this number to fifty and acquired estates to finance the enlarged establishment. The old minsters must by now have become inconvenient and it would clearly be more suitable to have one much larger church. According to the Worcester Annals work began in 1084 and by 1089 the new church was sufficiently far advanced for the monks to move into it. This must mean that within five years the crossing and the eastern bays of the nave, together with the presbytery and the crypt beneath, were completed. William of Malmesbury says that 'When the work of the main church, which he had begun from the foundations, had advanced to that stage of growth that now the monks might move into it, the old church which blessed Oswald had built was ordered to be unroofed and destroyed.' This suggests, though it does not prove, that the old church lay in the area of the present nave or cloister.

It is significant that Wulfstan had a remarkably modern view of the destruction of ancient buildings, saying; "We miserable people have destroyed the work of saints, pompously thinking we can do better: how much more eminent than us was St Oswald who built this church; how many holy men of religion have served God in it."

In spite of this he pulled Oswald's church down.

We do not know when the rest of the church, that is, the western part of the nave, was completed, but presumably it was part of the building campaign which added the cloister and the monastic buildings, including the chapter house, in the early years of the 12th century. We know nothing, at present, about the Anglo-Saxon monastic buildings which these new buildings replaced.

Wulfstan's church was constructed in pale Cotswold limestone and in green Highley sandstone and was simple and massive, and there is ample evidence that it was largely white-washed both inside and out. A small fragment of the outside of the Crypt was found in the recent excavations there and shows that the masonry, though fine, was plastered, whitened and false-jointed, that is, had joints drawn on it in dark paint (fig. 8A). Areas of similar though later false jointing can be seen at the western end of the choir at triforium level (figs. 8B and 8C) - from the ground they are almost completely deceptive.

Apart from the Crypt, enough fragments of Wulfstan's church remain to enable us to say with certainty that his church was as wide as the present church, the nave was as long, and the tower and the western transepts were the same area as those which replaced them. The front endpaper shows the positions of these surviving parts of the early Norman Church and figs. 8-14 and 18-21 are photographs or drawings of most of them.

For example, fragments of evidence which prove that the first Norman church was as long as the present church are two column bases preserved on the outside of the west door, itself rebuilt in the 12th century. These survivals show not only that the Norman church was the same length but that the doorway was the same width, as it has been shown to be in the North Porch (figs. 11 and 12).

As a result of these fortunate survivals, we have been able to draw a conjectural reconstruction of Wulfstan's church, (fig. 15) which, while perhaps not exact in all its details, must give a close impression of its scale and its massive simplicity - a great white building, by far the largest in Worcester,

*Fig 8A. Fragment of the exterior plinth of Wulfstan's church, revealed in the Crypt excavations of 1986-7, showing the plastered and whitewashed wall with false-jointing.*

dominating the City. Its absence of external decoration contrasts sharply with that of the Gothic Cathedral which replaced it – compare for instance, our reconstruction of Wulfstan's tower with the present 14th century tower (fig. 76).

*Fig 8B. Part of the Norman Choir arcade incorporated into the wall of the Early English Choir arcade.* Photograph by Chris Guy.

*Fig 8C. Part of the Norman gallery arcade embedded above 8B in the Early English Choir triforium. The massive half-drum respond seen in Fig 16 lies on the other side of this wall.*
*Much of the apparent stonework here is false-jointing painted on plaster in an attempt to mask the junction of the Early English and Norman masonry, with the 14th century tower pier just in the picture on the left.*

*Fig 9.* *The west wall of the North Transept showing a large rectangular blocked window space, presumably of the 14th/15th century, which had been cut into the Norman wall which abuts the stair turret on the extreme right. The plain wall, which would have been plastered, is of coursed rubble construction unlike the turret which is of fine ashlar with banded masonry at the bottom. The possible significance of this difference is discussed on p.000.*
*At A is the scar of the vault which held the gallery of Wulfstan's Church whose floor was at the level of the string course at B. At C is a window converted from the door which led from the stair turret out on to the gallery.*

19

*Fig 10. The north east corner of the north west Transept showing fragments of earlier walling and, at D, the springing of an arch of the 11th century gallery.*

*Fig 11. A surviving attached shaft E of Wulfstan's church, (at D on front end paper) contrasting with the 14th century shafts F beyond.*

*Fig 12. The North Door of the Cathedral showing the two attached shafts C,C with plain capitals and bases (below floor level) showing that the North Door of Wulfstan's church was here and was the same size as the present door. The rest of the doorway and the Porch date from11386, though the whole front was taken down and rebuilt in the 19th century restoration.*
*There is documentary evidence (quoted in Felicitas Corrigan,* The Nun, the Infidel and the Superman *p.36) that there was a large porch over the 11th century door, in which the cantors, four or five monks and boys, had stood to sing the* Gloria Laus.

*Fig 13. The northern base of the West Door showing the twelfth century base, A, above the buried 11th century base, B, revealed here by excavation.*
Photograph by Helen Lubin.

*Figs 14A and B. Capitals from the arch between the South Transept and the former East Transept chapel, now the John Chapel. Their date is a matter for discussion but is between 1100 and 1120 and based on Anglo-Saxon models.*

Fig 15 *Reconstruction of Wulfstan's church* by Peter Scholefield.

In addition to the fragments visible in the church, a recent excavation in the north choir triforium revealed an almost complete respond, massively semi-circular in section, with a capital which is clearly of Wulfstan's period (figs. 16 and 17). This was an unexpected discovery and shows that the gallery to which it belonged must have been very like that surviving at Gloucester, though the Worcester gallery is some years earlier.

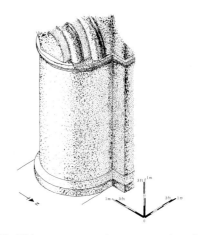

*Fig 17 is an axonometric reconstruction of the respond.*
Drawing by Chris Guy.

*Fig 16. The semi-circular respond or half-pier of the gallery of Wulfstan's church found embedded in the 13th century wall of the triforium on the north side of the Choir. The simple capital is similar to that of the central column of the Chapter House. Short drum columns like this are found in the gallery at Gloucester. It is probable that the columns of the Chancel of Wulfstan's church were also drum shaped, anticipating those of Gloucester, Hereford, Tewkesbury and Malvern.*
Photograph by Chris Guy.

Internally, Wulfstan's church, though the same size, was very different from the present cathedral. Dr Richard Gem has shown that instead of a triforium at first storey level it had galleries which ran round the whole church (figs. 18 and 19). In fact, recent excavations near the tower piers have revealed massive square bases which supported vaults covering the whole areas of both transepts (fig. 20). In effect, this first Norman Church was of two storeys, the extra floor space used principally to house chapels and altars.

Fig 18.   The east wall of the South Transept, showing, at D, the remains of one of the arches of the Norman Gallery, above the arch into the John Chapel, E.The wall was remodelled in the Perpendicular style.

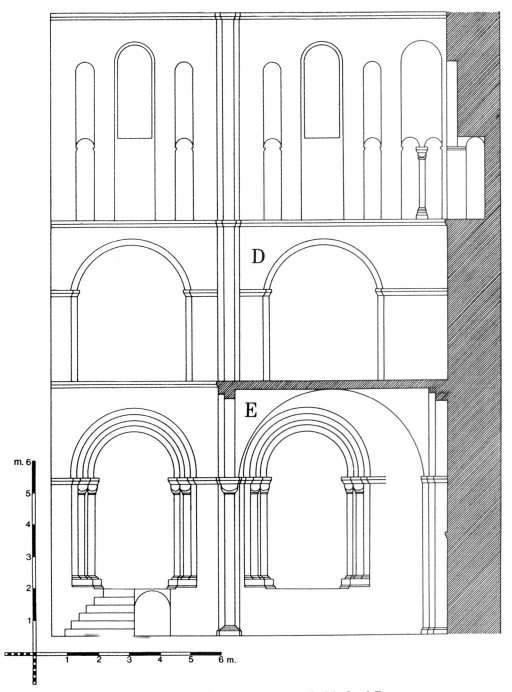

*Fig 19. Reconstruction of original internal elevation of east wall of the South Transept.*
(by courtesy of Dr Richard Gem)

While there were massive columnar piers in both storeys of the chancel east of the crossing, the nave arcade was composed of compound piers, that is with groups of attached shafts, two of which can be seen in the second piers from the west end of the Nave (fig. 20). In the excavations of the tower piers, the massive foundations of Wulfstan's time were found to be bluntly cross-shaped so it is probable that the piers of the Nave were cross-shaped also. The galleries of the Nave had double openings above the Nave arches and while the Chancel was very probably barrel vaulted, the Nave almost certainly had a wooden roof.

*Fig 20.  A pier of three dates – the pier in the north arcade between the 14th century bays on the right and the two late 12th century bays on the left, showing the remains of the pier of Wulfstan's church, with banded masonry in the centre.*

*Fig 21.   Excavations at the foot of the central tower of the Cathedral.*

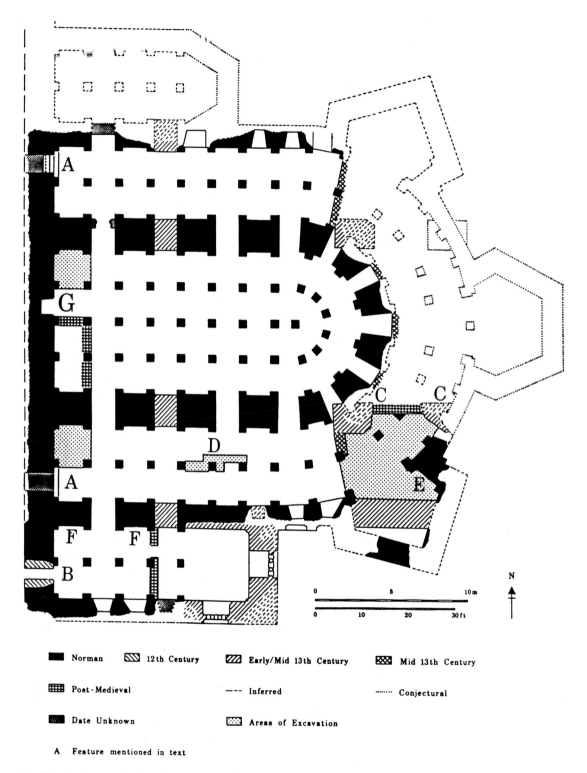

**Fig 22.** *The Crypt, showing the later alterations and the sites of excavations.* Drawn by Chris Guy.

Norman    12th Century    Early/Mid 13th Century    Mid 13th Century

Post-Medieval    --- Inferred    ....... Conjectural

Date Unknown    Areas of Excavation

A  Feature mentioned in text

# The Crypt

The Crypt is perhaps Worcester's chief glory, in spite of medieval (and more recent) mutilations.

It consists, as can be seen from the plan, (fig. 22), of a nave of seven bays and an apse supported by a forest of free-standing columns with plain or simple cushion capitals.

An ambulatory ran round this central nave but the apsidal end of the ambulatory was blocked-off and filled in during the construction of the new east end and Choir in the years after 1224. At the same time, some of the spaces between the original square piers were filled in to give greater support to the new Choir above. The filled-in parts can be distinguished from the original piers by their lack of chamfered plinths.

Beyond the ambulatory on the north and south sides were flanking chapels. The eastern end of the southern chapel was rebuilt in the 13th century with a square end and a ribbed vault. The northern chapel was destroyed at an unknown date, though no later than medieval times, and no traces of it are now visible.

Excavations in 1974 showed that there had been a radiating pentagonal chapel on the south side of the apse; it is presumed that there was a similar chapel to the north. A central chapel, on the east-west axis, is also presumed, although no evidence for this has been seen (fig. 22).

The original doorways into the Crypt led from the north and south transepts down short flights of stairs into the Crypt's aisles (A,A on fig. 22). These seem to have gone out of use at an early date, perhaps after the fall of the tower in 1175, being replaced at the south end of the south transept by the present door, B, which is 12th century in character. Presumably there was a door in the similar position on the north side, now obscured by the monument to Bishop Hough.

At the west end of the Crypt nave is a round arched opening, G, which appears to have been some form of cupboard. The interior has been badly damaged.

The primary purpose of the Crypt was to act as a place of worship and in a monastery with fifty monks many altars would be needed, some of which would have been in the Crypt. The documentary evidence shows that there were never shrines in the Crypt (as there were in some other churches) although there was an altar dedicated to St Peter. The archaeological evidence also supports the view that there was no shrine in the Crypt, as the floor of the ambulatory showed little sign of the wear which would have resulted from the feet of thousands of pilgrims.

Excavations in 1986-87 added information to those of 1974. They showed that two fine ashlar piers, C,C, had been inserted when the new Choir was being built and that these were intended to be free-standing and that the ambulatory was to be retained. However large cracks in these piers suggest that serious structural problems were encountered during the building and that it was then that the ambulatory was blocked off and filled in to provide greater support for the choir above, thus sealing the eastern end of the Crypt with whatever chapels and altars it had, and perhaps making the Crypt itself largely redundant.

*Fig 23.    The Crypt.* Photograph by Helen Lubin.

The excavation revealed that the soffits of the transverse arches of the vault had been painted with orange paint and that this was all the decoration the Crypt, or at least this part of it had, until the painting of the south side apsidal chapel with simple flowers and false jointing in the late 12th or early 13th century (see fig. 55 below).

Close examination of the free-standing columns of the Crypt shows that many of them were damaged and, more significantly, worn, before being used in the Crypt (figs. 25A and B) and that the original mortar overlies the wear. This suggests that they had been re-used from an earlier building (as much of the masonry in the eastern slype certainly has) perhaps from St Peter's, whose presbytery was enlarged in c.1040 or later. Many of the capitals and abaci are also ill-matched and some show the sort of damage that would occur if they had been removed from another building. While there is general agreement that the columns may have been re-used, there is considerable art-historical resistance to the suggested re-use of the capitals, as there is no recorded use of such capitals in England before the Conquest. Here the art-historical evidence appears to be at odds with the archaeological evidence and the discussion continues.

*Fig 24.  On the left a free-standing column and part of the vault of the Crypt as revealed in the excavation for the new staircase. The soffit, or underside of the transverse arches, A, of the vault, were painted with light orange-red paint, apparently the only original decoration of the Crypt. In the centre, the blocking wall of c.1230 inserted when the ashlar pier on the right, B, began to crack.*

In 1984 a short shallow trench, D,  was dug to   investigate the foundations of the free-standing columns in the south aisle (see figs. 27 and 28).  This showed, unexpectedly, that the columns did not stand on a sleeper wall or on a concrete raft, but on blocks of rubble which raised the column bases some 23cms. (9 ins.) above a concrete raft whose limits could not be seen in such a small trench.  One of the rubble fragments used to pack the bases was a segment of Anglo-Saxon archi-tectural ornament (fig. 28), the only piece of Anglo-Saxon sculpture yet recovered from the earlier Cathedrals.  It is datable to the ninth or tenth centuries.

Against the north-eastern wall of the apsidal chapel was found a mortared stone cist (E on fig. 22) containing the disarticulated remains of a man in his forties.  Radio-carbon dating of the bones showed that he had died be-tween AD 550 and AD 1030, but most likely in the late eighth or early ninth centuries.  He was probably an Anglo-Saxon nobleman, reburied here after his grave was discovered during the original building of the Crypt (see the exhibition in the Crypt).

Figs 25A and B. *Capitals in the Crypt showing the very thick joints, one packed with lumps of limestone, and the damage and wear which had occured before the shaft was used.*

Fig 26. *View of part of the excavation of the Crypt ambulatory for the insertion of the new staircase in 1986, showing an attached shaft and base, partly robbed away, and the original whitewashed plaster of the walls, both dating to 1084. Behind is one of the ashlar piers, C, of the new Choir of 1230.*

Fig 27. *Base of free-standing pillar in south aisle of Crypt, showing rubble packing which raised the base of the pillar above a concrete foundation, perhaps an earlier floor. One of the rubble fragments is a piece of Anglo-Saxon sculpture (Fig 28).*

Fig 28. *Photograph of a fragment of Anglo-Saxon sculpture with interlace and a bunch of grapes. Perhaps from a chancel screen. 9th or 10th century.*

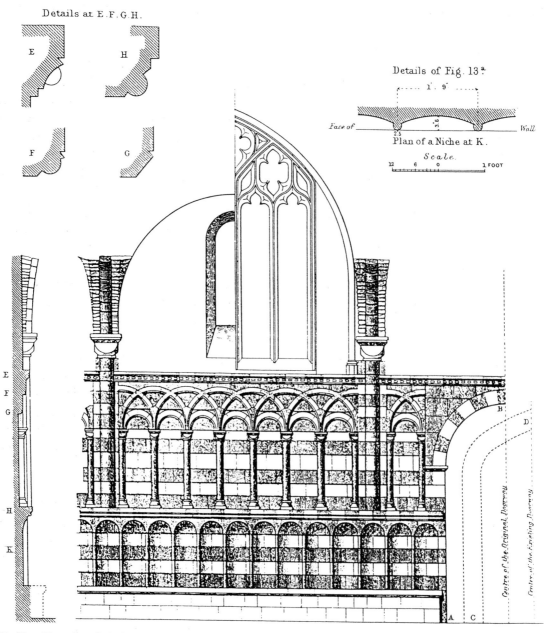

Details at E.F.G.H.

E    H

F    G

Details of Fig. 13ª

1'. 9'

Face of      Wall
2.5    3.6

Plan of a Niche at K.

Scale.
12    6    0      1 FOOT

Centre of the Original Doorway

Centre of the Existing Doorway

*Fig 29.    Elevation of one bay of the Chapter House showing the relationship between the Norman windows and the windows which replaced them in the 14th century (from Willis, 1862/63).*

## The Chapter House

The Chapter House is in some ways an optical illusion - polygonal and Perpendicular on the outside but circular and Norman within. The Norman work probably dates from 1100-1115 and certainly before 1125, and is the earliest of such circular or polygonal chapter houses, which appear to have been exclusively British - the majority of chapter houses being rectangular, a shape perhaps more suited for their purpose as the daily meeting room for the Chapter, with an eastern apse or other focal point for the Abbot, which the Worcester room lacks though it has been suggested that the circular shape is ideal acoustically.

A stone bench (hacked off in the 18th century to accommodate bookcases) ran round the base of the wall and provided 95 seats, more than ample for the 50 monks of Wulfstan's enlarged monastery. Each seat was backed by a round-headed niche, with above these niches a zone of intersecting blind arcading. This Norman work is patterned in alternate courses of white Cotswold and green Highley stone and is consistent throughout the room and was clearly meant to be seen and therefore was not initially painted or whitened. However, on the northern side of the room there are considerable traces of drapery painted directly on to the stone and covering both the white and the green courses, so that at an unknown date, but presumably in medieval times, and perhaps during the 13th century alterations to the Chapter House (see below), the banded decoration was effaced. By the 19th century the whole interior had been covered in whitewash which was removed in the restoration of the 1860s.

The vault is supported by a central column, and consists of ten radiating semi-circular ribs which stand on slender shafts dividing the outer wall into ten compartments each of which originally contained a single round-headed Norman window. Evidence for one of these has survived the late 14th century rebuilding and can be seen in the treasury passage to the north (fig. 29). The vault is built of tufa, for lightness, and originally had an elaborate scheme of paintings, now lost, but which are described in a document (MS F81) in the Cathedral Library (*Worcs. Cath. Notes* etc. 1909-1914 and see below.)

Though the design of the Chapter House was a *tour de force*, the weight of the vault and its roof gradually thrust out the walls, particularly to the east and south, where they are not supported by adjacent buildings. As a result, the building was remodelled in the late 14th century, although there is some evidence that it may have been extensively repaired before that. The central pillar has a base which is 13th century rather than Norman in style, and the pillar itself is similar to the 13th century choir piers in construction. Although the capital appears to be early Norman it may be re-used and partly rebuilt and the evidence suggests strongly that the central pillar and therefore the vault, were repaired or reconstructed in the 13th century, at about the time of the building of the new choir. It may be that the vault was completely underpinned while the central column was replaced, perhaps because the column had failed. Alternatively, the whole vault may have been dismantled and rebuilt with a new column. If this was so the vault paintings would have been destroyed in the process, and they had certainly gone when Willis saw the vault stripped of its whitewash in the mid-19th century.

Fig 30.    The central column of the Chapter House and the springing of the vault. The capital, though perhaps reset, is typical of Wulfstan's time. The column itself may be 13th century.

Fig 31.    The interior of the Chapter House, showing the central pillar, perhaps rebuilt in the 13th century, the blind arcading of c. 1100-1120 and the blind windows (blind because they abut the south transept) of the late 14th century. The vault was remodelled at that time to take the enlarged windows.

Fig 32. The 'waterholding' base of the central pillar of the Chapter House, presumably 13th century in date. It is this base which has caused a great deal of discussion leading to the suggestion (among others) that the vault was either completely rebuilt or supported by scaffolding while the pillar was rebuilt at some time in the 13th century.

Fig 33. The door of the Chapter House seen from the interior, showing the earlier blocked Norman doorway A, on a different alignment, the new four-centred door being built to fit the vaulting bays of the cloister outside.

## The Eastern Slype
(T on the front end paper)

The eastern slype which led through from the cloisters to the monks' cemetery, is a curious anomaly. It lies between the Chapter House and the southern wall of the south transept, and so is presumably contemporary with them, yet it is almost entirely built of re-used Anglo-Saxon masonry - bulbous bases, and capitals that appear to be 'lathe-turned', with re-used attached columns - fragments without doubt of one of the Anglo-Saxon churches demolished to make way for Wulfstan's new building. Even the blind arcading is made up of small re-used voussoirs crudely put together. Only the capitals on the south side, which are similar to those in the Crypt, appear to be new. While the demolished earlier churches were undoubtedly re-used as rubble or re-cut as ashlar in Wulfstan's church, these are the only fragments that are visible. The ledge on which the blind arcading stands is equally irregular with a chamfered plinth in two places but rough uncoursed masonry elsewhere. The whole passage is very different in construction from the other surviving parts of Wulfstan's church, but the explanation is probably now beyond recovery.

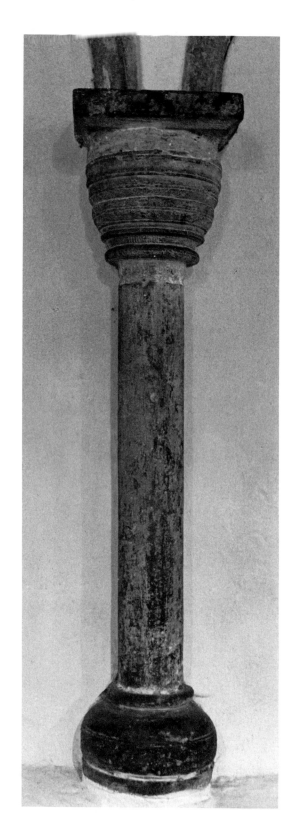

Fig 34.   Detail of the blind arcade of the eastern slype showing a re-used Anglo-Saxon capital and base.

Fig 35.   The groined vault of the eastern slype.

Fig 36.   The northern blind arcade of the eastern slype showing the re-used Anglo-Saxon voussoirs, capitals and bases.

*Fig 37. The east walk of the Cloister, showing the cupboard recesses, now housing redundant bells. The monastic library was probably here until the mid-14th century when it was moved to its present position.*

The east walk of the Cloister includes two large rectangular recesses, at present housing the redundant bells, which probably held cupboards for the books being used by the monks working in the Cloister Scriptorium, while the west walk includes the monks' lavatorium or wash-place. This was fed by a lead pipe, over 2000 yards long, which brought water across the river from the Henwick Road. This lavatorium has clearly been reset at some time since the ends of the water trough are now blocked off by the 14th century vaulting shafts with a third shaft inserted half way along its length.

*Fig 38. The north wall of the Cloister – the outside of the south wall of the Nave – showing the massive plain Norman buttresses. Note that the 14th century vaulting bays of the Cloisters are spaced in an entirely different rhythm.*

*Fig 39. The Cloister west walk with the lavatorium in the foreground. This has presumably been rebuilt as the water trough is cut across by the 14th century pier for the Cloister vault and its ends are blocked off.*

Fig 40.  The Refectory from the east end showing the Norman Undercroft with its flat buttresses and small roundheaded windows. The corner buttresses are additions of the 14th century and the east wall has an inserted late 14th century window with flowing tracery.

Fig 41.  Christ in Majesty. A great sculptured panel of the early 13th century at the east end of the Monastic Refectory (College Hall) showing the seated Christ in a mandorla, a lobed oval space, surrounded by the symbols of the four Evangelists and flanked by niches which presumably held figures of Saints. There are traces of paint, particularly red paint, in the backgrounds. It was hacked flat after the Reformation, perhaps at the same time as the same treatment to the reredos in Prince Arthur's Chantry. The friezes above and below are of the 14th century.

## The Monastic Buildings

The monastic buildings are outside the scope of this book, except to draw attention to the ruins of the dormitory, its undercroft and its reredorter (or latrine) with a deep drain which emptied into the river. These buildings, together with the infirmary, which has completely disappeared, lay between the west end of the Cathedral and the river. This westerly site was an unusual position for the dormitory which normally lay over the Chapter House on the eastern range of the cloister, with a night staircase giving access to the south transept for the first service of the day. The unusual shape of the Chapter House with its tall conical roof precluded this, and Worcester's monks had to walk the whole length of the nave to get to their choir.

## The Refectory

The Refectory (now called College Hall) takes up the whole of the south range of the cloisters. It was originally a Norman first floor hall of great size standing on an undercroft, which still exists, though much altered. The undercroft has flat buttresses and small round-headed windows to the south, and has a groined vault supported by a central row of squat piers. The three central piers are cylindrical with simple capitals suggesting that these central bays had a different function from the two ends.

The north wall, that is, the cloister wall, is very thick with buttresses of two sizes, and with two large blocked Norman arches. The main 14th century doorway into the hall is here, towards the west end, while there is a smaller doorway into the undercroft, which has been extensively remodelled in this area.

In medieval times, the original doorway into the undercroft appears to be that still existing in the southern slype leading into the cloisters.

The doorway into College Hall on the south side, though 14th century in style, is new work of the 19th century and recent excavations there have shown that it partly blocks an original Norman window and that there was no door here at ground level in Norman times, though there may have been one subsequently at the level of the hall, reached by a wooden staircase, to give access to the kitchen.

The hall itself was entirely rebuilt or drastically remodelled in the 14th century, but it was also extensively modified in the 19th century so that much of the original work is obscured; it is possible that the upper walls are basically Norman. It is hard to see why the building should have been dismantled down to the top of the undercroft without very good reason, and this is not apparent, though it has been suggested that the original upper floor here (and of other buildings, such as the infirmary), may have been of timber or timber-framed, perhaps with stone gable walls.

Inside the east end of the hall are the mutilated remains of a magnificent over-life-size Christ in Majesty surrounded by the symbols of the Evangelists (fig. 41). The date of this is c.1220-1230, that is, the date of the beginning of the rebuilding of the east end of the Cathedral, though the friezes below are 14th century additions. This great sculpture was presumably built into the east end of the Norman refectory and re-used and re-framed when the hall was remodelled.

*Fig 42. The Undercroft of the Refectory showing the rough vaulting which has lost its original plastering. This would have been similar to that which survives in the eastern slype. Two of the apparent scalloped capitals are fragments of decorated string-courses.*

The whole building, and especially its undercroft, have been drastically altered and mutilated and is perhaps the least studied and least understood of the whole cathedral complex and deserves detailed survey. One important anomaly mentioned above, for which there is no immediate explanation, is the fact that the refectory is not aligned with the cathedral or the rest of the monastic buildings, but lies at about 5° to them. It is possible that this reflects the alignment of other buildings, standing then, but long since gone. Only excavation will solve this problem.

# 4.   THE LATER 12TH CENTURY

The work on Wulfstan's original plan for the monastery appears to have continued until at least the end of the first quarter of the 12th century and perhaps beyond.

However, in 1175 there was an event which, however interpreted, marked a setback and caused considerable rebuilding. An entry in the Worcester annals under that year says: *Nova turris Wigorniae corruit*, 'The new tower of Worcester fell'.

This laconic comment poses some difficulties, principally the position of the fallen tower.   Willis thought it was the crossing tower, but Brakspear suggested that the tower which fell was one of a pair at the west end and opinion is still divided . However, the excavations at the foot of each crossing tower pier, made in the 1980s to examine the foundations before the tower's restoration, showed unequivocally that there had been a second tower, sandwiched in time between Wulfstan's original tower and the present 14th century tower (see figs. 43-45). This makes it extremely probable that it was the central tower which fell in 1175 and was renewed, incorporating re-used Romanesque masonry, soon afterward, eventually being replaced in the 14th century.

However, why should a tower which fell in 1175 be called the *nova turris*, since Wulfstan's original tower was presumably built soon after 1084?  One possible answer to this question is that the original tower was squat, rising only a little higher than the surrounding roofs, and that the 'new tower' had been a heightening of the first tower and it was this addition, made a short while before 1175, that had collapsed. This would fit the excavated evidence.  It has been objected that there is too much original Romanesque masonry surviving at the west end of the Choir for it to have been the central tower which collapsed, but if it were only a low tower being heightened it may (as with other towers, notably at Chichester) have collapsed vertically, falling inwards on itself and doing little damage to the surrounding masonry.

The transept first floors nearer the crossing may well have been damaged or destroyed when the tower fell. There was undoubtedly remodelling of the transepts at about this time with the removal of the galleries and the chapels opening out of them at first floor level.

For example, surviving fragments of later 12th century work can be seen in the south transept and there are splendidly ornate late 12th century blind windows in the same transept's south wall, though these are now barely visible behind the case of the great organ.

The argument that it was one of a pair of western towers which fell in 1175 has been supported by the fact that the two western bays of the Cathedral were completely re-

# WORCESTER CATHEDRAL · South West Tower Pier · NE angle
## Interpretation

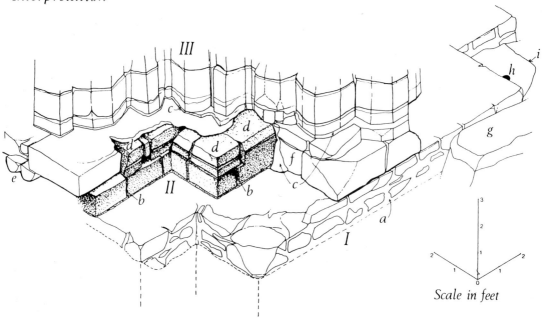

Scale in feet

*Fig 43.   Axonometric drawing of the excavation of the south west Tower pier. The excavation at the base of the pier showed conclusively that there were three phases of construction: first, a massive base of uncoursed rubble, clearly, for reasons which there is not space to detail here, the Norman foundations of c.1084. On this stood a foundation which, at first sight, appeared to have a chamfered plinth of Norman date and to be contemporary with the base below. However, closer examination showed that the stones of which it was constructed (d) were, in fact, reused abaci from capitals or string courses paralleled exactly in the nearby crypt of 1084, but here reused upsidedown. Mortar samples were taken from joints at a and b, examined and compared and shown to be different from one another. Mortar samples from joints in the fourteenth century pier at c were also examined and proved to be different again. Clearly there were three phases of construction. However, it was also seen that the fourteenth-century pier, which was a different shape from the underlying bases, had itself been packed with reused Norman architectural fragments, including a column drum, f, and a double capital, e. g is a floor, probably of the first period, which has sunk and tilted, while h is a posthole, perhaps for a scaffold pole, set in a pit, i. The probable sequence of events is thus: the building of the first Norman tower, I, after 1084 and perhaps as late as 1150s; the collapse of this tower and the building, after 1175, of a second tower, II, on foundations derived from the collapsed masonry; the building of the third tower, III, in the late fourteenth century, again reusing Norman masonry, but this time probably from the destruction of the ambulatory of the crypt when the east end of the cathedral was rebuilt in the thirteenth century.*

*Fig 44.   The foundation of the south west Tower pier. Compare with the drawing, Fig 43.*

built at about that time, a date based on stylistic grounds. Whatever the force of the argument, it is clear from the architectural evidence that these two bays replace two earlier bays and were not an extension to the nave. First, the two piers (B, B on the front end paper) are each of three phases, the northern and southern shafts part of Wulfstan's church of the 11th century; the western shafts of the late 12th century and the eastern shafts of the 14th century. It can been seen that the 11th century shafts are semi-circular and therefore must have been part of a pier and not part of a western wall. It is also worth commenting that the use of white and green stone in these piers is not consistent, as it is in the chapter house, which suggests that here as well as in other parts of the early Norman church which have survived, where the stonework is equally random, it was not meant to be seen but was white-washed.

The two western bays, built as they were in the last quarter of the 12th century, and perhaps as early as 1175+, are 'Transitional' in the sense that they combine round-headed and slightly pointed arches in the same design (for instance, the triple clerestory arches are pointed-round-pointed). The early Norman gallery or tribune has been replaced by a narrow triforium, blocked off from the roof space behind except for doors in the centre of each bay, and with a tripartite arrangement of semi-circular arches, zig-zag decorated, with the central arch stilted, all contained within a pointed arch. The blank spaces within the arches are filled with individual paterae curiously shaped like whorls of cake icing.

Fig 45.  *Fragments of Romanesque masonry, including a double capital (e on Fig 43), used as rubble in the foundations of the second tower, c.1175-1200, and discovered in the excavation of the south-west Tower pier in 1981.*

Fig 46.  *A bay of the late 12th century west end of the Cathedral. Notice the blank round-headed window behind the 19th century font.*

The main arches of these two bays are slightly but elegantly pointed and the capitals throughout are variations on the trumpet scallop and crocket types, except for the capitals on the high vaulting shafts, which are richly decorated with foliage, one (fig. 49) harking back to the original Corinthian capital from which these capitals ultimately derive. They are hardly appreciated without binoculars.

The ribbed vaulting in the corresponding two bays of the south aisle is contemporary and very fine; it is probable that the compartments, or severies, between the ribs were once plastered and whitened also. In the south wall are two simple blind round-headed windows, which were probably matched by real windows in the north aisle. However, this aisle and its windows were largely rebuilt in the 14th century, though the wall shafts were retained.

*Fig 47. One of the capitals of the late 12th century western bays of the Nave, showing the awkward adaptation of the triple-shafted capital to the attached column of the 11th century pier (in white) below. Beyond, on the right, are the shafts and capitals of the 14th century Nave arcade (cf. fig 71).*
Photograph by Chris Guy.

*Fig 48. The triforium of the two late 12th century western bays, showing the stepped arches with zig-zag decoration in the centre and the curious applied whorls, resembling cake decoration, called* paterae. *Notice the mixture of round and pointed arches in this transitional style of c.1175-1200.*
Photograph by Chris Guy.

Fig 49.   One of the high capitals of the two late 12th century western bays of the Nave. Photograph by Chris Guy.

Fig 50.   The scalloped trumpet capitals of the late 12th century piers of the two western bays of the Nave, a logical development of the capitals in the Crypt. Notice the imaginative variety of the designs and the way in which the concave abaci and the undercut trumpet shapes enhance the play of light and shade on the capitals. Photograph by Chris Guy.

*Fig 51.    The late 12th century vault of the two western bays of the South Aisle showing the mixture of round and pointed arches of this transitional period. The vault between the ribs would have been plastered and whitewashed – the present rustic appearance with careful pointing is 19th century.*

Fig 52. *The exterior of the late 12th century bays of the Nave showing, at A, a blocked Norman window, possibly circular, replaced by a Curvilinear Decorated window, renewed in the 19th century.*

Fig 53. *The late 12th century west door, largely rebuilt in the 19th century refurbishment. The masonry of the 12th century in the lower parts of the doorway can be distinguished from the 19th century masonry by its different tooling. The wooden boxes at A,A, cover the fragments of 11th century bases which prove that the west door of Wulfstan's church was here and of the same width.*

*Fig 54.  The 12th century door at the east end of the Refectory which opens into the southern slype leading from College Green to the Cloister.*

# 5. THE PAINTED DECORATION OF THE LATER 12TH AND 13TH CENTURIES

So far as we can tell the interior of Wulfstan's church was plain and white, as the Crypt and the eastern slype are now, with the only evidence for added decoration the orange paint on the soffits or undersides of the arches in the Crypt, and some fragments of plaster with red parallel lines which may be from the upper parts of his church. If the windows were of plain glass (and there is no evidence at present of stained glass here at this date) the building would be full of reflected light, much more like a vast non-conformist chapel than the present interior, which depends for its decoration on the light and shade of modelled and sculptured stone, some of which was itself originally painted.

However, it is now clear that in the late 12th and early 13th centuries the interior of Wulfstan's church was transformed by great schemes of wall and vault paintings. Some still survive fragmentarily on the walls, for others we have archaeological evidence, while for some we have only documentary evidence.

The chief evidence for the decoration in the main body of the Cathedral comes from the large quantity of painted plaster debris found in the Crypt excavations of 1986-87, while we have documentary evidence for the schemes in the Chapter House, and the 'Maccabees' series.

However, these colourful paintings do not seem to have survived for very long, being swept away in the rebuilding of the east end in the years after 1224, in the probable rebuilding of the Chapter House vault, and in general the change from areas of whitened wall and vault which formed an ideal support for paintings, to a multiplicity of columns, much larger window space and a new emphasis on light and shade which left little room for painting except on the vaults.

We do not know what decorative schemes there were on the Norman tower and nave piers and walls but they may have been extensive, eventually being destroyed in the the 14th and 15th centuries when the tower and nave were rebuilt.

In addition to the still visible remains of wall-paintings, traces of paint can be seen on the sculptured figures which fill the spandrels of both the choir and nave triforia. The backgrounds against which they sit have also been painted, apparently with washes of red. No doubt may other sculptures, capitals and bosses as well as these were painted or gilded.

The Victorian scraping was ruthless and must have removed much still extant painting though some bosses have since been repainted and regilded.

# Wall Paintings in the Norman Church

An we have seen, the original decoration of the Crypt was shown by the 1986-87 excavation of the staircase to be simply orange paint on the soffits of the transverse arches. The excavation of the apsidal chapel revealed, however, that it had been decorated with false jointing and flowers with curving stalks (fig. 55). A 13th century date is suggested for this painting by parallels with very similar decoration in the chancel of Martley Church, 6 miles away, where the decoration continues into the splay of a pointed and therefore presumably 13th century window. However, since this end of the crypt was destroyed in c.1240 for the building of the new choir, the painting must have been carried out only shortly before it became redundant. There are similar paintings, with single flowers, on the capitals at the entrance to the chapel at its western angle, though these are now difficult to discern.

During the excavations for the construction of the new staircase into the Crypt the tons of rubble which filled its abandoned east end were carefully sorted and a large quantity of painted wall plaster was recovered from the lowest levels of the filling, plaster which with very little doubt was derived from the destruction of the Norman Chancel above.

Determined attempts have been made to fit together these many fragments, with comparatively little success, since presumably they represent only a very small proportion of the total original paintings. However, some clues to the decorative schemes can be deduced and these will be published in due course, but undoubtedly the most important fragment is the face of a saint or angel (fig. 56). This extraordinarily beautiful painting has been provisionally dated to the later 12th century. It is remarkable for the reflection in

*Fig 55. Wall painting, probably of the late 12th or early 13th centuries, in the southern apsidal chapel of the Crypt, uncovered by the excavations for the new staircase here. It consists of wide false-jointing with simple flowers and thin stems. The blank area in the centre of the photograph is perhaps the site of an altar, or a memorial. As can be seen, the false jointing on either side is not aligned.*

Photograph by Helen Lubin.

the eye and the sensitivity of the mouth, which go beyond the stylisation of much contemporary painting. It is perhaps related to a now lost painting of an angel with a censer, which was found in the jamb of a window in the Crypt 'destroyed to make way for the new foundations' in 1860. This angel was copied at full size and in colour before being destroyed but the copy has recently and very unfortunately disappeared, though not before being photographed (fig. 57).

## Two Lunettes

On the north wall of the western end of the southern Crypt chapel are two painted lunettes so badly damaged as to be almost indecipherable (F,F on fig. 22). The more westerly of the two has traces of two figures, the right hand one a ?bishop with the lettering S. TOMAS - presumably St Thomas à Becket rather than the doubting disciple.

*Fig 56.* *Fragment of wall-painting found in the Crypt excavations of 1986-87.*

*Fig 57.* *An angel with a censer. Copy of a wall painting found in the Crypt in 1860.*

Other letters are faintly discernible. The other lunette is more badly damaged but the outline of a trefoil filling the space and therefore framing whatever was painted in it, can clearly be seen. The trefoil presumably dates the painting to the late 12th century or later.

In the writer's opinion the decipherment and conservation of these paintings is a matter of real urgency.

**The Chapter House**

In the Cathedral Library there is a manuscript, F81, a 12th century folio of St Jerome, on the fly leaf of which is a series of verses entitled *Versus capituli*, implying that they were inscribed in a chapter house, and since the manuscript apparently originated in Worcester, probably the chapter house here.

A transcription of the verses will be found in James, 1913 and a translation will be found in Wilson, 1913 (both in *Worcs. Cath. Notes* etc. 1909-1914). There are ten verses, which correspond to the ten bays of the chapter house, and they are preceded by a set of lines headed *in circuitu domus*, which Wilson suggests were painted 'in rather large capitals on a band of stonework running all round the Chapter House, and probably below the paintings ...' (where there would have been space before the windows were enlarged in the 14th century rebuilding).

The subjects were taken from the Old and New Testaments and were arranged in symbolic groups. By remarkable coincidence there is an illuminated manuscript in the Library of Eton College, which contains a series of pages containing roundels, with verses round their edges, ten of which coincide almost exactly with the Worcester verses (Henry, 1991). It seems very likely therefore that the two manuscripts are related and that the Worcester Chapter House was painted with roundels very similar, if not identical, to those in the Eton College manuscript, though there are five roundels and two separate half-roundels on each page of the manuscript, whereas the Worcester manuscript describes only four roundels to each 'bay'. It is suggested that each compartment of the ten-sided vault contained four roundels, disposed as in the accompanying sketch by Brakspear (fig. 58) who suggested this arrangement. This seems highly likely as there is no other space for them, even though the niches behind the encircling bench were eventually painted, though clearly not with roundels. It would be possible, using the Eton College manuscript as a model, to reconstruct in colour the vault of the Chapter House here as it was in the later 12th century - it must have been spectacular.

*Fig 58.*

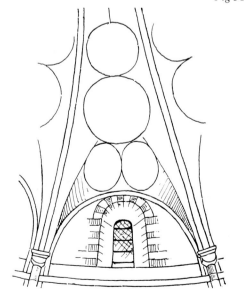

Of the niches (fig. 59), Willis wrote 'On the wall of the niches were traces of painting, of which black outlines remained. They were exactly the same in each niche, and represented an angel holding an expanded mantle, as in the old paintings of the stalls of St Stephen's Chapel, Westminster, but these figures were simpler, showing merely the head and part of the wings, with the hands above the mantle. As the niches are 4 feet high above the seat, the head and hands of the guardian angel would just appear over the head and shoulders of each monk when seated in his stall.'

There are also faint traces of painting on the central pillar, notably two spiral bands, which perhaps once held inscriptions.

## A Maccabees Cycle

In 1914 Canon Wilson drew attention to a manuscript in the Library of Clare College, Cambridge MS KK5.6, on a fly-leaf of which, in handwriting of about the first half of the 13th century, is a series of Latin verses describing pictures illustrating the story of the Maccabees (Wilson, 1914 in *Worcs. Cath. Notes* etc. 1909-1914).

Wilson argues that the scheme of paintings described in the above MS was on the vault and perhaps also on the south wall of the western slype, (now, in 1994, the Cathedral Gift Shop). Though there is no proof of this, Wilson saw traces of paint along the ribs of the vault before they were removed by work-

*Fig 59.   The traces of painting in the niches of the Chapter House seating, said to be of angels holding up their robes. Note that the painting has been applied directly to the stone (without plastering) and that it crosses the banded stonework which had originally been intended to be seen.*

men without further record (on 17th September 1914). It is possible, however, that these paintings which he describes as 'scenes of war and bloodshed' may have been in the Guesten Hall (e.g. see p.80 below) or in the Refectory or the Cloisters.

# 6. THE NEW EAST END

King John died at Newark in 1216 and, following a request made in a codicil to his will, his body was brought to Worcester and buried before the High Altar. Two years later the church, completed after the rebuilding of the two western bays and the collapsed central tower, was dedicated in the presence of the young King Henry III, and the body of St Wulfstan was translated into a shrine.

It is surprising, therefore, that only six years later, in 1224, Bishop William of Blois with his master mason, Alexander, replanned the whole east end, beginning with the construction of the Lady Chapel and eastern transepts outside the Norman apse in the monks' graveyard, followed by the demolition and rebuilding of the Norman Chancel.

The reasons for this drastic remodelling are not clear but may be connected with the promotion of the cult of St Wulfstan and the encouragement of pilgrimages to his shrine and to that of St Oswald, which lay together, with King John's tomb between them[N]. There is also the recorded collapse of two small towers in 1222. Although the positions of these towers are not known, if they were at the east end, they may have weakened the structure or destroyed sufficient of it to suggest total rebuilding.

The new design removed the galleries of the Norman east end and replaced them with triforia. Since the galleries had almost certainly contained altars, space for these could now be found in the extended eastern arm and the new transepts.

The work on the new building began in 1224 and may have continued until 1240 - 1250. William of Blois died in 1236 and was succeeded by Walter de Cantelupe who continued the work on the Choir. There is a visible break in the construction between that part - the Lady Chapel and the eastern transepts - which lay outside the Norman building and the part which replaced the Norman chancel and apse. Willis describes the differences in the design of these two parts in detail (*op. cit.* 1863). It is at the junction of the two phases of construction that problems arose which resulted in the demolition and filling- in of the ambulatory of the Crypt (page 29 above).

The new east end is in the Early English style with pointed arches, tall narrow windows, a marvellous variety of stiff-leaf capitals, (which contrast sharply with the plainness of the previous Norman capitals) and the use of black Purbeck marble shafts to contrast with the Highley stone used in the rest of the building (figs. 60-63).

The arcades, triforia and clerestories of this new building were different in their proportions from the Norman chancel, as can be seen from the fragments of the earlier church

N. It is suggested by Mr Michael Craze that John's tomb and the two Saints' shrines lay along the axis of the church rather than laterally.

*Fig 60. The south east transept which illustrates the 'unrestrained verticalism' of which Pevsner speaks (1968 p.302). Attached Purbeck marble shafts run from the top of the blind arcade straight through to the vault, only punctuated by the annular rings which attach the shafts to the structure.*

*Fig 61. The east end of the Cathedral with the south eastern transept and Prince Arthur's Chantry on the right.*

Fig 62.  The vault of the Lady Chapel and the eastern transepts crossing (painted by Hardman in the 19th century restoration.

Fig 63.  The south arcade of the Choir. The blind arcade at the back of the triforium has spacing which is out of step with the arcade at the front. Purbeck marble is used throughout for free-standing, clustered and attached shafts of great delicacy.

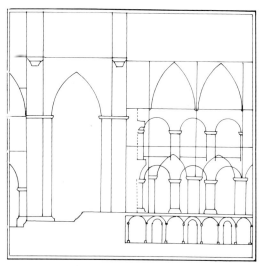

which remain (fig. 64), and as Willis points out, the Lady Chapel arcades are narrower and higher than those of the Choir (because the Choir floor has to be higher over the Crypt) giving 'the Lady Chapel ... a grandeur and loftiness of appearance greatly superior to that of the choir, whose arches appear sprawling in comparison ...'

The emphasis is on verticality throughout. To quote another enthusiastic admirer of this building, 'what conveys that irresistible excelsior to the Lady Chapel and the Transepts is that, though the windows are in two tiers, Purbeck shafts run up all the way' (Pevsner, 1968, 303).

*Fig 64. Elevation of the Tower arch and the eastern side of the Choir showing the relationship between the Crypt, the Norman arcade and the Gallery above with the 13th century arcade, triforium and clerestorey.*

*Fig 65. Plans of the Norman Crypt and the 13th century Choir superimposed to show their relationship.*

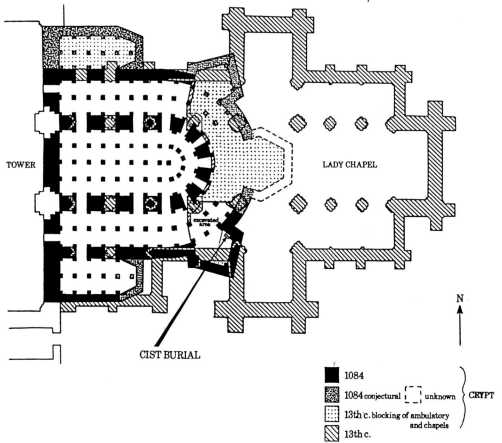

TOWER

LADY CHAPEL

N

CIST BURIAL

- ■ 1084
- ▨ 1084 conjectural
- ⌐ ⌐ unknown
- ⸬ 13th c. blocking of ambulatory and chapels
- ▨ 13th c.

CRYPT

*Fig 66.  Part of the vault of the Choir, painted by Hardman. The panel of blind arcading on the left was painted by Helen Lubin to fill an area left blank by renewal of the plaster.*

*Fig 67 over.  The blind arcading of the south eastern transept (the Dean's Chapel) showing one of the spandrel sculptures – the Expulsion of Adam and Eve from Paradise.*

*Fig 68 over.  Sculpture in a spandrel of the north aisle of the Lady Chapel, c1224, very probably representing Bishop William of Blois presenting his newly rebuilt church at an altar. However, while the trefoil in the gable of the church and the cusped doorway behind him are 13th century in style, all the windows are round-headed, i.e. Norman and therefore anachronistic. The southern of the tomb effigies on either side of the altar in the Lady Chapel has a similar beard and moustache, and is also probably William of Blois, though there is confusion, in both the labelling and the literature, between him and the northern effigy, which is almost certainly earlier, and therefore not Walter de Cantelupe, who did not become Bishop until 1237 and died in 1266, then being buried before the High Altar.*

The ribbed vault has longitudinal as well as transverse ribs and the painted scheme throughout is by Hardman (fig. 66). The two eastern transepts and the Lady Chapel have blank pointed-trefoil arcading running round the whole east end, but this does not continue westward into the choir aisles. The capitals of this blind arcading are all stiff-leaf crockets and the spandrels contain sculpture of great variety: foliage, little animals and monsters and figures and, most interestingly, little religious scenes: The Angel sounding the Last Trump; the Resurrection, with the dead climbing out of their graves; the Expulsion from Paradise; the Tortures of Hell; the Annunciation; the Visitation and the Nativity (fig. 67). One of the sculptures in the north aisle shows William of Blois offering a model of his new church to an altar in an act of dedication (fig. 68). This image has been used as a logo in the current restoration appeal.

*Figs 69 A to G.   A series of crocket and stiff leaf capitals from the east end of the Cathedral.
As the building progressed from east to west the capitals became increasingly complex eventually
becoming smaller and more naturalistic in the Crossing and the Nave (Figs 71 and 72, B and C).*

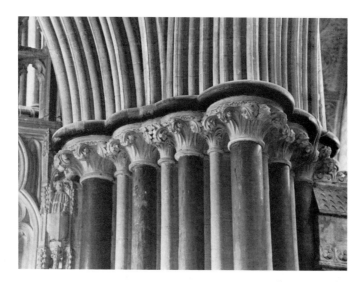

Much of the extreme east end was rebuilt in the Early English style by Perkins in the 1860s as part of the great refurbishment, restoring to it something of the unity it must have had in the 13th century (see chapter 9 below).

We can try to envisage the Cathedral as it was when the new east end was completed - the new Choir was attached to the second Norman tower and the transepts, though modified, were still Norman; the main part of the Nave was probably still as it was in Wulfstan's time, though perhaps with painted decoration and the two western bays were late  Norman, as they are now (see fig. 46). It was probably not a coincidence that Worcester's great Antiphoner, including music going back to Oswald's episcopate, was collected together at this time, the building of the new Choir.

Fig 70.    The east end of the Cathedral showing the way in which Perkins married his new East End with the original 13th century arcade of the Lady Chapel.

# 7.  THE 14TH AND 15TH CENTURIES

After the completion of the Choir, probably by the middle of the 13th century, there seems to have been a pause in the rebuilding until c.1317-20 when the north arcade of the Nave and the north aisle were rebuilt in the Decorated style, with flowing tracery in the windows (especially elaborate in the Jesus Chapel) and with complex piers with capitals of leaves more bunched and realistic than the stiff-leaf capitals of the Lady Chapel

*Fig 71.    The North arcade of the Nave, built c.1317-20, seen from the west.*
*The vault was added c.1377.*

*Fig 72A.    The tierceron vault of the Nave, built c.1377.*

and the eastern parts of the Choir's, but seeming to develop from the capitals of the Choir's western piers.

The north aisle was vaulted by Thomas Cobham, Bishop, c.1327, though the triforium and clerestorey of bays 3 and 4 (counting from the west) are in the Perpendicular style as is the whole of the southern arcade and aisle vault and the inserted windows in the south (Norman) wall. Here the bases are different from those on the north, and the capitals are separate and of thinner leaves.

*Figs. 72 B and C. B shows one of the Decorated capitals of the Nave arcade with continuous abaci and bold clustered leaves, in comparison with the Perpendicular capitals at C which are separate and smaller allowing the mouldings to run up between them, emphasising the verticality of the design.*

In spite of the time between the rebuilding of the north and south arcades of the Nave, which span the transition between the Decorated and Perpendicular periods, the styles of the two arcades, though subtly different, are sufficiently similar to preserve the unity of the whole. Whether this is due to innate conservatism on the part of the Worcester masons, or a conscious desire to unify the design, we have no way of knowing.

During the rebuilding of the Nave and the aisles, the Norman roof, which was presumably of wood, not vaulted in stone, must have been removed and the Nave left open to the sky until both arcades were completed, when it was vaulted, in 1377[N]. This was at the same time as the building of the Library, in the south Nave aisle roof space and the Dormitory (now destroyed).

N. It is of course, possible that the roof was completed some years before the vault was begun.

*Fig 73. The north range of the Cloister and the external wall of the south aisle with the windows of the Library above. The window tracery of the Cloister is 19th century, by Perkins, the aisle windows are late 14th century Perpendicular of an elaborate kind, while the rectangular two-light windows above are of the mid-15th century, probably of the time of Bishop Carpenter, (1444-1476) to give more light to the Library. The clerestory windows above are obscured by scaffolding while the roof is being repaired (summer 1993).*

Meanwhile in 1320 Prior Braunston built the Guesten Hall; the Edgar Tower was completed in 1368-69; the Refectory and the Cloister were rebuilt (on Norman foundations) in 1372, and the tower built (or begun) in 1374 and its vault over the crossing constructed in 1376. In 1378 the Water Gate was built and in 1379 the Infirmary and the Choir Stalls; in 1380 the west window (now, of course, replaced) and in 1386 the North Porch.

In addition, at some time in the late 14th century, the Chapter House was drastically remodelled, with new, enlarged windows of early Perpendicular style between deep thin buttresses (fig. 89). The external surface of the thick Norman wall was cut away and refaced, reducing the weight of the walls, and the vaults over the windows changed from low and semi-circular to high and pointed, transferring the thrust of the vault on to the new buttresses.

*Fig 74. The interior of the Library, mid 15th century.*

This remarkable and very costly spate of building began in c.1317 and went on, apparently continuously for 70 years. The dates given here may be the dates at which the work was begun, or on which they ended, since such a programme must have meant overlapping work on the major contracts, but whichever they are, they give the relative chronology and enable us to see how the work alternated between the monastic buildings and the church, culminating in the North Porch.

It is worth pointing out that the quality of the Guesten Hall and the Refectory show that the monastic buildings were as architecturally important and imposing as the Cathedral itself.

In 1504 Prince Arthur's Chantry was constructed, the last addition to the Cathedral Church before the Dissolution of the Monastery.

*Fig 75. The east face of the Edgar Tower, the entrance to the monastic precinct. Originally built in the 14th century (completed in 1368-69) it was heavily restored in the 19th century refurbishment. The statues date from this time but the great wooden doors are original.*

**The Tower**

*Fig 76.   The central Tower seen from the south. In spite of being drastically scaled in the 18th century, rebuilt in the 19th and lacking its pinnacles along the balustrade, it has retained its original proportions and remains a splendid monument, dominating the landscape for many miles around.*

As we have seen, the present tower is the third on the same foundations. We know little about the second tower, except that it was based on the foundations built for Wulfstan's tower, but packed with re-used Romanesque masonry. The third, present tower, that of 1374, has piers which are diamond shaped in plan, and unexpectedly, were found to oversail the rectangular Norman foundations. The four complex piers soar up to pointed arches at the same height as the Nave and Choir vaults, which gives an extraordinary unity to the interior, unbroken except by Scott's lacy screen which serves only to mark the break between the western and eastern halves of the church - Nave and Crossing; Choir and Lady Chapel.

The tracery of the upper part of the tower is Decorated, of the lower Perpendicular, a curious anomaly not easily explained. The central part of the tower was originally intended to be open, without a vault, forming a lofty lantern which would have made the crossing extraordinarily light and airy, but this seems to have been abandoned at an early stage, and the present vault inserted.

*Fig 77. The interior of the central stage of the Tower showing the large openings, now blocked. Photograph by Chris Guy.*

*Fig 78. The Crossing, showing the tierceron vault under the Tower with elegant cusped decoration at its centre. The whitening of the compartments is recent and enhances the pattern of the ribs. It would almost certainly have been whitened originally and perhaps decorated with paintings.*

At some time after the construction of the Nave arcades, flying buttresses were inserted into the two eastern bays next to the tower, presumably because of some fears of, or actual, movement of the tower. The two buttresses are not identical, and may have been inserted at different times. That they were not built with the arcades is shown by the straight joints in the work and the slight differences in the stone (figs. 78A and 78B).

Fig 78A. *The flying buttresses inserted into the north arcade triforium and clerestory to support the tower pier seen to the right.*

Fig 78B. *The flying buttresses inserted into the south arcade triforium and clerestory to support the tower pier seen to the left. Subsequently, due presumably to further problems of stability, the thicker curved buttress was inserted into the triforium of the second bay.*
*Since the four original buttresses appear to be contemporary, they are all later than the completion of both arcades c.1377. Note that while the triforia of both arcades are similar the clerestory of the later south arcade has triangular arches in contrast to the four-centred arches of the northern clerestory.*

## The Guesten Hall

The Guesten Hall was a five-bay ground floor hall, built in c.1320, with some of the most elaborate Decorated windows with flowing tracery in the whole Cathedral complex (fig. 80). It had a splendid five-bay roof with tiers of cusped and curved windbraces, dated 1326 - 'the most elegant of medieval carpentry in the county' (Pevsner, 1968, 322). When the Guesten Hall was demolished in 1862 because money could not be found to save it, happily the roof was kept, modified and used on Holy Trinity Church at Shrub Hill. When that church in turn was demolished the roof was preserved, and taken to the Avoncroft Museum of Buildings, near Bromsgrove, where it is now displayed over a new sub-structure (fig. 82).

South-west View in 1861

*Fig 79. An engraving of the Guesten Hall made in the year before it was demolished. The porch with its upper door is already in ruins. Note also the ruined building joining the Hall to the Chapter House. (from the Hore collection).*

*Fig 80. Internal elevation of the Guesten hall. Compare with the same view photographed in 1993 (Fig 81). Note that the doorway is round-headed, not pointed as in the engraving and that a later inserted door has been blocked. (from the Hore collection).*

*Fig 81.	The east wall of the Guesten Hall, all that now remains. It dates from c.1320 with what must have been fine flowing tracery in the windows. The two left-hand windows end high up in the wall, because there was a building behind, perhaps a kitchen. There was also a Prior's lodging beyond. The roof (Fig 82) is now at the Avoncroft Museum of Buildings at Bromsgrove.*

*Fig 82.	The arched braced roof of the Guesten Hall, c.1320, as it is rebuilt at Avoncroft Museum of Buildings, Bromsgrove.*

## The Cloister Vaults

The Cloister was rebuilt in the 14th and 15th centuries, beginning with the east walk. The doorway from the church at the north-east corner is c.1300 while that at the north-west corner is Perpendicular. The vault has central octagons of lierne ribs, though the west walk differs in its details. The most striking feature is the rich variety of bosses in all the walks. In the east walk they are small, mostly of leaves and heads, but the south walk has the finest bosses, of figures and scenes culminating in the centre with the Coronation of the Virgin. The west walk has leaf bosses, while the north walk has applied figures of angels (fig. 86). It is possible that this walk was vaulted last, because of the new work in the south aisle of the church. It is not clear how much of this vaulting was painted though it is very probable that the bosses and figures were polychrome, and the severies, or compartments, white-washed to give greater light. This is not now obvious, though detailed examination may determine whether any colour has survived the weathering of the stone and the Victorian scraping.

An 1866 description says: 'Some of the groinings which are of a different coloured stone, are very fine, and a few in Bath stone ... appear almost as perfect as if they were carved a twelve months ago ... some are so dilapidated as to be indistinguishable. The best (preserved) appear to be in Caen stone, or in some limestone closely resembling it. Those which have crumbled away are in Highley sandstone (New Red) or in North Cotswold Öolite, which is of variable quality'. In other words, the varied state of preservation is due to the variety of stones used in the cloister vaults (fig. 85).

The window tracery throughout is by Perkins, who replaced tracery of the 18th century.

*Fig 83.  The east range of the Cloister with the Chapter House beyond.*

*Fig 84.    The lierne vault of the south walk of the Cloister.*

*Fig 85.    Sculptured bosses in the south walk of the Cloister showing the Tree of Jesse. Notice the remarkable preservation of all but one of these sculptures, due to the stone used. The nearest boss, probably of Highley stone, has almost eroded away, while the others, perhaps of Caen stone, are nearly perfect and show varied discolouration which may be the remains of paint.*

*Fig 86.    The lierne vault of the north walk of the Cloister with many angels carrying shields. The date is perhaps
c.1377, the date of the Nave Vault.*

*Fig 87.    The lierne vault of the South Aisle of the Nave, probably dating from about 1377, the date of the Nave Vault.*

*Fig 88.    The Monastic Refectory (College Hall) and the Chapter House seen from College Green. Note the Undercroft with a 12th century door to the right (the pointed-arched doorway on the left is 19th century). The Hall above was considerably modified in the 14th century, with large Decorated windows, heavily restored in the 19th century.*

*Fig 89.    The exterior of the Chapter House, seen from the south east. The upper walls, above the string course, have been cut back to make them thinner, and the large windows, with Perpendicular tracery, inserted replacing the original smaller Norman windows. The lower walls have also been cut back, only less so, and the buttresses and parapet added transforming the exterior from Norman to Perpendicular.*

*Fig 90. The North Porch. This 14th century porch replaced a porch, probably of the same size, of Wulfstan's time. Wulfstan's porch, like that still existing at Tewkesbury, may have been barrel-vaulted. The whole front of this porch was taken down and rebuilt in the 19th century restoration and the statues all date from that time. There are rooms above the porch, now used by the Cathedral Architect and Archaeologist.*

Fig 91.   The east wall of the north west transept showing the original Norman arch into a side chapel, (now destroyed) and the 14th century arch which replaced its pair into the choir aisle. Above, the wall has been transformed into the Perpendicular style by the addition of panelling, Perpendicular windows, and a decorative quatrefoil parapet under the clerestory.

Fig 92.   The painted decoration of the 14th century arch into the north choir aisle, consisting of rosettes and painted zig-zag ornament reminiscent of Romanesque ornament. Between the attached shafts below can be seen the ghost of a crocketed canopy.

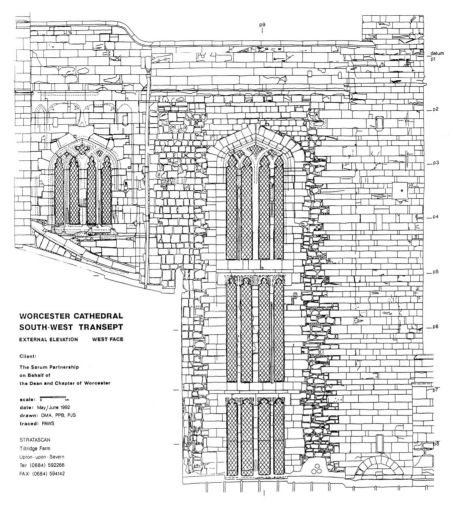

WORCESTER CATHEDRAL
SOUTH-WEST TRANSEPT

EXTERNAL ELEVATION    WEST FACE

Client:

The Sarum Partnership
on Behalf of
the Dean and Chapter of Worcester

scale: 0 ___ 1m
date: May/June 1992
drawn: DMA, PPB, PJS
traced: PAWS

STRATASCAN
Tiltridge Farm
Upton-upon-Severn
Tel: (0684) 592266
FAX: (0684) 594142

Fig 93.    Stone by stone drawing of the
           west face of the south west
           transept.

Fig 94.    Interpretation of figure 93.

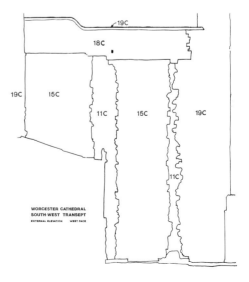

## The Water Gate

The present Water Gate dates from 1378, and excavations there in 1993 suggested that it is the first structure on the site, though the Severn has undoubtedly been used for river traffic since Roman times, if not before, and there is some evidence of an early crossing-point here. Until the mid-nineteenth century the river was tidal, so the Water Gate would flood twice a day, forming a small dock into which boats could be brought for unloading.

A ground-probing radar survey carried out on the landward side of the Gate on the road which slopes up to College Green appears to confirm the suggestion that there was a slipway up which boats could be hauled through the Gate and up the slope, probably by means of a winch. Excavation here might confirm this.

The Gate has two archways, the inner rebated for a pair of doors, with their hinges still in place; the outer with a portcullis slot that continues 1.1m (3ft 6ins) below the present road level. This portcullis slot implies that there was a building above the Gate, presumably also of sandstone and probably crenellated, tall enough to house both the portcullis when it was lifted and the winch necessary to lift it (fig. 95).

This gate is more heavily defensive than the Edgar Tower, the gateway from the City into the precinct, and suggests that the precinct was felt to be more vulnerable from this side, or perhaps that valuable cargoes needed protection - these were the years of the Peasants' Revolt.

Excavation has shown that the southern wall which extends from the Gate towards the river is 2.4m (7 feet 10ins) deep at the towpath end, and has not only graffiti below present ground level but iron rings for tying up boats. This wall, which appears at first sight to be Victorian, must be earlier than the creation of the towpath on this side of the river. Pictorial evidence suggests that this was before 1823, so that the wall is probably late 18th century in date.

The inner walls of the Gateway have a mass of graffiti on both sides (though unfortunately no dates) among them the life-size outline of a salmon, caught here in perhaps 1813 or, less probably, in the 1840s.

Fig 95.   *The Water Gate from the river, which is in flood, showing the depth of water which would have filled the Gate at high tide. The conjectural outline of the upper storey housing the portcullis machinery has been superimposed on the present house.*

# Prince Arthur's Chantry

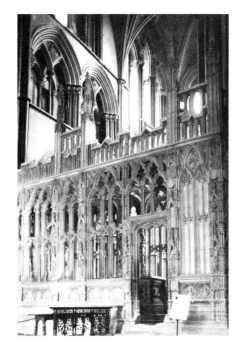

Fig 96.   *Henry VIII's elder brother, Prince Arthur, died in 1502 and this Chantry was built in c.1504 to house his tomb. It is in the Late Perpendicular style with much openwork, including the decorative crenellation. There are many heraldic symbols and figures of Angels, Saints, Kings and Bishops in canopies.*

Fig 97.   *On this, the south side, the tomb is lower than on the north and incorporates two earlier, 14th century, monuments to members of the Giffard family, seen at the bottom of the photograph.*

*Fig 98. The interior of Prince Arthur's Chantry showing the lierne vault with pendants, and the wonderfully elaborate reredos with the Deposition of Christ at its centre, carved flat after the Reformation so that it could be covered with painted plaster.*

*Fig 99.   The Nave (from Wild 1823) showing the Perpendicular stone screen with organ above which blocked off
the Choir and Chancel until Perkins and Scott opened up the vista in their reorganisation of the interior.*

# 8. DECAY AND RESTORATION FROM THE 16TH TO THE 19TH CENTURIES

At the Dissolution of the Priory, in 1539, many of the minor monastic buildings were converted into houses for the new Prebendaries and Canons and other ministers of the new foundation, but the greater monastic buildings probably survived unaltered until the Civil War.

On the feast of the Assumption in 1537, the Shrine of Our Lady of Worcester had been despoiled and her jewels, coat and shoes had been taken away.

In 1538 the shrines of St Oswald and St Wulfstan were taken down and their relics buried at the north end of the High Altar (it is said wrapped in lead with the bones of Bishop Cantelupe). An excavation there in 1971 failed to find them.

On January 10 1547 'Images were destroyed over the whole church.' The usual practice seems to have been to destroy completely statues that were within easy reach, or to knock off their heads. Others more inaccessible often survived. By and large, only those statues considered idolatrous, such as those of Christ, the Virgin Mary and the Saints were attacked. The fine sculptures in the spandrels of the eastern transepts and the misericords, for example, were left untouched.

In 1551 the Choir was moved from its position two bays west of the Crossing to its present position. At the same time a platform which extended under the Crossing and into the eastern two bays of the Nave was removed.

The Civil War brought considerably more destruction to the Cathedral and its monastic buildings. On Saturday 24 September 1642 the Parliamentary troops under the Earl of Essex entered Worcester as an occupying army and on the next day, Sunday 25, an orgy of desecration and destruction began in the Cathedral. Service books, vestments, windows and statues were destroyed, horses were stabled in the Nave and Cloisters and camp fires lit, and the Choir and Aisles were used as latrines. The occupation only lasted a little over a month, but the damage done to the building and its furniture is incalculable.

In July 1646 Worcester again fell to the Parliamentarians after a long seige and in 1647 it was decided that a 'leaden steeple in the Cathedral Churchyard' then used as a wood-house 'should be stripped of its lead, which should be sold for the re-edification and repair of Almshouses and churches'. This steeple was, without doubt, the detached bell tower which stood close to the Cathedral on the north east side. Probably at about the same time, roof timbers and lead were stripped from the east transept with its lead pinnacle, the vestries or south chapels of the Choir, the Chapter House, the Dormitory, the Cloister, and the Gate House (presumably the Edgar Tower). At the same time the lead conduit pipe which brought water from Henwick Road to the Lavatorium in the Cloister, a pipe no less than 2140 yards long, was removed and the conduit houses and a lead cistern destroyed.

The document drawn up by Canon Barnabas Oley which lists this destruction is dated 6 November 1660, soon after the Restoration of the Monarchy, and suggests that it was made in preparation for repairing the Cathedral and the major buildings at least, since they would rapidly deteriorate without their roofs.

There is also evidence that it was at this time that Charles II restored the Cathedral rents in order to provide money for the repairs and upkeep of the Cathedral and its ancilliary buildings.

Major repairs were carried out from 1712-1715 when £7000 was spent, an enormous amount at the time. The outer walls were cased and the pinnacles at the corners of the central tower were rebuilt, while the interior was strengthened with inserted walls and arches.

The tall spires, which are shown on engravings of that date (fig. 100), but not on Dugdale's view of 1672, must have been added at about that time.

*Fig 100. The Cathedral (from Wild 1823) seen from the north-east showing the tall pinnacles and flying buttresses removed by Perkins together with the Decorated style window of 1792.*

The sacrist's lodging, which was built outside the west end of the north Choir aisle, was taken down, but the oriel window, inside the church, which gave the sacrist a view into the interior from his house, can still be seen (fig. 101).

Another major campaign of repairs, which lasted for eight years, was carried out between 1748 and 1756 when the north end of the North Transept was rebuilt. The great flying buttresses at the east end were built between 1736 and 1789 (fig. 100), while the window at the west end was rebuilt in 1789 and that at the east end in 1792 (fig. 102).

*Fig 101. The oriel window of the Sacrist's lodging, seen inside the north choir aisle. From here the Sacrist could keep his eye on the High Altar and the Sanctuary.*

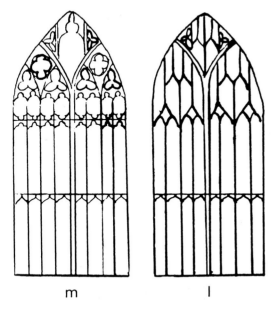

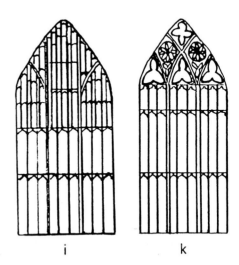

| m | l | i | k |

l    Old west window. Erected 1380.
m    New window. Erected 1789.

i    Ancient east window.
k    New window. Erected 1792.

*Fig 102. Showing the old east and west windows and their 18th century replacements which were swept away in the 19th century restoration.*
From Valentine Green, *Worcester,* Vol. I (1796).

*Fig 103. The east end of the Cathedral (from Wild 1823) with King John's Tomb in the foreground, showing the 18th century east window (seen from outside in fig. 100) and the screen behind the High Altar (seen in fig. 106). Engraved in 1863, after the east window had been altered but before the new reredos was built in 1877.*

The great Tower was scaled several inches deep at about this time, by which, as Willis says, 'its architectural character was greatly injured'. A new Altar Screen and a new Choir Screen were set up in 1812; the tall pinnacles were taken down some time after 1832, and, finally, in 1857, the major restoration was begun under the direction of Abraham Perkins, the Cathedral Architect, who had the foresight to leave a part of the Cathedral (in the north Choir Aisle) untouched, to show succeeding generations, including us, the state of the building as he found it, weathered and broken and covered with whitewash, (fig. 105). Whatever our opinion of the drastic Victorian Restoration, the Cathedral could not have been left as it was, run-down and patched up with temporary expedients. As Willis says 'in the interior, settlement of the piers and arches in the Early English work [that is the Lady Chapel and Choir] had attained so alarming a magnitude as to threaten the stability of the structure'. And the walls and arches inserted in 1712 were themselves giving way 'having served rather to change the direction of the settlements than to stop them' while an article on Worcester in *The Analyst,* Vol ii, p. 98 1835 begins 'perhaps no English Cathedral presents so heterogeneous an appearance, in its external aspect, such a patched and threadbare coat of many colours, presenting so little to admire, and so much to deplore as the Cathedral at Worcester.'

*Fig 104. The Choir in a print by Wild of 1823 showing the ?18th century Choir stalls with their elaborate wooden colonnades and the great organ above the screen. The medieval Choir stalls seem to have been swept away, though the misericords, which still exist in their original positions, must have been incorporated. The pulpit on the right dates from 1642.*

*Fig 105. Two tombs in the North Choir Aisle, deliberately omitted from the Victorian reconstruction to show the state of the Cathedral as Perkins and Scott found it – broken and eroded and covered with white-wash.*

# 9. THE VICTORIAN RESTORATION

In spite of large sums spent on the Cathedral between 1818 and 1834, when expenditure only fell below £500 twice and was often nearer £1000, Thomas Rickman wrote in 1833 ' I find the music meeting is to be held in the Cathedral now though I do not say the roof will fall I do say that I think it dangerous to have the music meeting there with the Groining in the state it is in or would I myself go to the Cathedral on the occasion.'

But such awful possibilities are belied by John Britton's contemporary view of the Nave where the triennial music festivals were held (see fig. 99).

Sir Robert Smirke, consulted in the same year, thought that the chief problem was with the structure of the main roofs, where the timbers had parted company with the walls, but that if these roofs could be repaired, a small permanent work force could deal with the other problems of the fabric. By 1845 a local architect, Abraham Perkins, had become Cathedral Architect and he began the general restoration in 1857. He was joined by George (later Sir George) Gilbert Scott in 1864. It is these two men together with the Ecclesiastical Commissioners' Architect, Ewan Christian, who were responsible for the drastic alterations, amounting in some cases to complete rebuilding, which give the Cathedral much of the character it now has. This character is not being altered by the present restoration which is being carried out on entirely different principles (see Chapter 10 below).

Perkins removed many late medieval, 17th and 18th century features, including window tracery, screens, buttresses and pinnacles, completely demolished and rebuilt a large proportion of the east end, and took down much of the central tower and remodelled it. Most of this restoration and renewal was due to the condition of the fabric, which had suffered from the fact that in the past a great deal of vulnerable, easily weathered stone had been used. Many inappropriate piecemeal additions were properly swept away, but at the same time, there was a continuous and sometimes acrimonious debate, not on the structural solutions to be adopted, but on the architectural styles which should be used in the areas of rebuilding. It is interesting to see that attitudes towards late medieval, 17th and 18th century work changed during the course of the restoration, but in general most post-medieval work was considered 'bad'.

For example, in 1853-54 the Ecclesiastical Commissioners asked Ewan Christian to report on the fabric. While he thought that 'the main features of the architecture are in all parts still clearly distinguishable and especially in the earlier portion are extremely beautiful' he nevertheless wrote that three windows of the choir clerestory 'have been filled with course (sic) tracery executed in Higley (sic) stone and are in every respect of the worst possible character ....' However Perkins had already gone ahead and begun to replace them to match the original Early English work still remaining at the East End.

Fig 106. *The Lady Chapel in 1863 after the insertion of Perkins' new 'Early English' windows but before the screen was replaced by the present reredos in 1877.*
(Engraving in The Builder 1863)

Fig 107. *The Chancel with the High Altar and the Reredos. This illustrates clearly the unity achieved by Perkins and Scott, merging their new work with the existing 13th century building.*

In 1855-56 Perkins restored the Lady Chapel and demolished the south-east transept flying buttresses. It is typical of the confusion and disagreement surrounding much of the restoration that Ewan Christian thought that the buttresses were 'not later than the mid-fifteenth century'; Britton, who engraved views of the Cathedral, thought they were 15th century; Willis thought (after their demolition) that they had been 18th century, while Perkins himself calls them 'added'. However, since in 1686 some £200 was bequeathed towards buttresses to the Choir and Lady Chapel, they may, in fact, have been 17th century.

While Christian's report is silent on the question of the great east window, Perkins takes the opportunity of suggesting in a pencilled note on the report 'If the eastern gable be taken down [as Christian had agreed] won't it be advisable to replace the large window by a five-light lancet [i.e. Early English] window - which - or something similar - was probably there before the present ugly one?'.

The assumption was that the east and west windows were both late 18th century and therefore despicable. A Cathedral guide of 1854 describes the tracery and glass of the new east window erected in 1789 as 'very bad'. Informed opinion was clearly on Perkins' side and he rebuilt the east end accordingly and both Willis and Christian recorded their approval, Christian reporting that 'the effect of the building in its restored state is exceedingly beautiful'.

However, by 1862 opinion regarding the wholesale replacement of ancient windows and other features with modern copies of earlier styles was beginning to change and

Willis himself gave his view that there was no historical justification for an Early English window at one end of the great transept and a Decorated window at the other. Fortunately for Perkins, criticism was deflected by the controversy over the demolition of the Guesten Hall in that year.

Between 1863 and 1865 the new west window and door were built. The lower part of the west door is late 12th century and can be distinguished from the 19th century work by the character of the tooling, while below the 12th century bases the 11th century bases still remain in situ (fig. 53). Fig. 102 shows the successive 14th century and 18th century windows which were replaced by Perkins' Geometrical Decorated window.

In 1866 opinion had changed sufficiently for the *Saturday Review* to attack the work being done at Worcester: 'What then do we find this Dean and Chapter doing? They are letting loose a local genius to work his will upon the venerable walls, which other and better men have raised, and the form of which they themselves could never have distantly approached in conception ...'

As early as 1850 George Gilbert Scott had written 'an authentic feature, though late and poor, is more worthy than an earlier though fine part conjecturally restored - a plain fact, than ornamental conjecture'. By 1862 Scott was arguing for 'conservative' restoration - the philosophy of the present day.

In the case of Worcester, Perkins' views prevailed and a great deal of his restoration consisted, as we have seen, of rebuilding in close imitation of earlier medieval styles.

After 1864 the major restoration was that of the Tower which was strengthened in the hope that it would 'have the finest peal of bells in the country'. The outer walls were taken down perhaps as far as the main roofs, and the plans of the walls laid out on the floor of the Cathedral nave before the rebuilding.

While the style of the Tower was generally retained, early engravings and other evidence show that a number of details were altered, in particular, the silhouette was changed by the addition of 2 feet to the height of the parapet (which had small finials, now removed) and 7 feet to the height of the pinnacles.

The front wall of the North Porch was taken down and rebuilt in 1865 and Hardman and Forsyth supplied a complete new sculptural scheme. The ground outside the north side of the Cathedral was lowered at this time - the raised pavement outside the houses of College Yard shows by how much - and the cloister garth was lowered by 0.5m (1.5 feet).

In 1868 the structural restoration was complete, and Scott began the reorganisation of the interior (see figs. 108 and 109). He designed the sumptuous reredos and the screens, including the open screen in the style of the 13th century; the choir stalls (which, however, incorporate the marvellous series of misericords of 1379) and the choir organ cases. The nave pulpit, in the Italian style, was designed by Scott and carved by Forsyth. The stained glass throughout is 19th century, and will be the subject of a separate book, as will the very varied sculpture in the Cathedral.

The restoration was virtually complete by 1874, and the achievement was celebrated by a round of re-opening ceremonies, the first attended by some 3000 people, many of whom processed through the City with flags and banners. £114,295 11s 4d had been spent since 1840 and this huge sum, similar in its day to the amount being spent on the present restoration, put Worcester at the top of the restoration 'league table' published in *The Builder* in 1876.

*Fig 108.* *The north side of the Choir. Compare with fig. 104, a print dating from 1823. The screens, the canopies, the organ and the choir stalls are all by Scott, though the back rows of the choir stalls on each side are 14th century and contain a fine series of misericords of 1379.*

*Fig 109.* *The Choir Screen, by Scott. This open work screen which replaced the stone screen of the 14th or 15th century seen in fig. 104, enables the building to be seen as a whole from east or west instead of divided into separate spaces. As Pevsner says 'the greatest asset of Worcester is the unity of its interior.'*

Fig 110. *The east end with Perkins' east windows on the left and much original 13th century work on the right. The stained glass is by Hardman.*

Fig 111. *The east end of the Cathedral seen from the south with the south-eastern transept on the right. This shows the way in which Perkins married his new work with the original Early English east end, since only the clerestory is medieval.*

*Fig 112. The great West Window, 1863-65.*
Photograph by Chris Guy.

*Fig 113. Victorian splendour. The Reredos, designed by Scott and made by Farmer and Brindley.*

*Fig 114. The back of the Reredos, sumptuously decorated, the alabaster incised and painted in red and gold with a cross and the symbols of the Evangelists. Dedicated to Dean Peel and his wife, 1877.*

# 10. THE PRESENT RESTORATION

## BY KENNETH WILTSHIRE, CATHEDRAL ARCHITECT

Great buildings, such as the Cathedral, seem to require major restoration about once every century. The situation at Worcester is compounded because much of the local stone used in the medieval period was soft and friable, and quickly became eroded - see, for example, the exterior of the two western bays on the north side, which have lost all their detail (fig. 52). There has also been deterioration due to poor workmanship in the past, and particularly the use of iron cramps, some of great size, which have expanded with rust and cracked or shattered the stonework. In addition, two World Wars and the depression of the 1930s made extensive restoration programmes out of the question.

After 1945 isolated repairs were undertaken to the Cathedral of which the major related to the masonry of the Tower in the 1950s, the recovering of the north nave aisle, North Porch and Jesus Chapel in 1973 and the releading of the south nave aisle over the Library in 1981.

For the first time in very many years an overall view of the Cathedral was taken in 1986 following which a long term programme of work, extending throughout the buildings, was agreed.

Of prime importance was the stability of the Tower where regular monitoring of fractures in the four piers had taken place

*Fig 115. The west face of the south-west transept showing the condition of the rendering and masonry before repair.* Photograph by Helen Lubin.

over a number of years. The point of criticality was fast approaching and measures to strengthen and consolidate the piers were put in hand following the successful launch of an Appeal for £4,000,000. In order to achieve the work the Nave altar was moved to the west end of the Cathedral and the area around the tower piers completely screened off. Altogether some 1,400 holes were drilled into the columns to receive stainless steel bars penetrating deep into the core which was also grouted, pinning back the columns to a homogeneous load-bearing form (fig. 116). On the east side evidence was found of some degree of panic on the part of the 13th century masons carrying out the 'updating' of the Quire. Movement had obviously taken place during the course of the

work and the Norman triforium gallery was not entirely taken down where it abutted the Tower but very hastily filled leaving a certain number of voids. Similar evidence of rapid buttressing having to be taken was also found in the Crypt area when the new entrance steps were formed earlier (see chapters 3 and 6).

Almost all the roofs of the Cathedral were found to be in very poor condition and early stripping and recovery had to be undertaken to the two Lady Chapel aisle roofs which involved reformation, upgrading and improvement of the lead gutters and repairs to the timbers.

*Fig 116.*

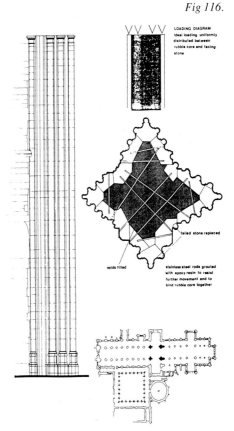

*Fig 116.  THE PROBLEM*

*The four tower piers support a load of some 4,200 tons; each column consists of a thin outer stone facing backed with rubble filling. Over the course of years the movement of the tower and breakdown of the very poor original mortar in the core had resulted in the latter settling and having a considerable number of voids within it. The result of this is that the load was being increasingly taken on the thin outer stone facing which was failing. This was evidenced by the distortion and bending of the piers and the cracking and general failure of a very considerable number of the facing stones.*

*The problem was recognised some ten years ago and a programme of careful monitoring of the cracks and failure was undertaken. Drawings were made of every stone in the columns and the positions of cracks marked at regular intervals. Tell-tales were inserted and read every month to indicate more accurately the aggregate movement.*

*Sections of the facing stone were cut out and the core withdrawn for examination. This enabled photographs to be taken by means of closed circuit television cameras of the inside of the columns. In February 1988 a radar scan was made around the columns to determine as accurately as possible in three dimensions the anomalies within the core. Previously the foundations of all columns had been exposed and happily found to be in good condition.*

*THE PROPOSALS*

*The core has now been reconstituted by a slow and careful process which involved grouting and the insertion of stainless steel cross ties together with the absolutely minimal amount of stone replacement possible.*

*The drilling and the insertion of rods was carried out carefully and in such positions so as to 'scar' the columns as unobtrusively as possible. Stone stoppers were used with very tight joints and toned down to match the colour of the adjoining stonework as closely as possible.*

*Above the level of the columns a number of Victorian iron ties within the tower which were rusting and which would eventually damage the stone and cause more problems were taken out. They were replaced by a combination of reinforced concrete beams and stainless steel cross ties set at key points which will help to contain and equalise the thrusts and movement from the bells and wind which inevitably occur within the tower.*

*Fig 117.  The north-west Nave aisle buttress showing the disintegration of the stone.* Photograph by Chris Guy.

Although the public appeal had been very successful it had always been realised that the Dean and Chapter would need to augment it to bring the total figure up to some £10,000,000 at 1986 levels in order to accomplish the whole of the necessary work. A policy decision was also taken that capital of at least £2,000,000 would be retained to fund future work and avoid, if at all possible, having repeated appeals. The programme of work was therefore devised in order to work within the funds available, leaving intact the capital sum mentioned above. Fortunately the implementation of grants for work to Cathedrals by English Heritage gave a substantial boost and, in spite of the constantly increased scope of work found necessary, enabled steady progress to be made. It was always essential to balance the proprieties of structural stability and public safety, since

*Fig 118. The Nave roof showing the rotted foot of one of the principal trusses.*
Photograph by Chris Guy.

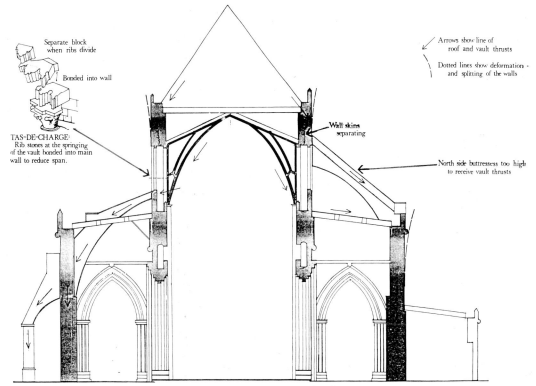

*Fig 119. Cross section through the Cathedral showing some of the causes of the major potential structural failures which the present programme of repairs is designed to correct.*

very large scale failure of the masonry was evident throughout the Cathedral, in a large part due to the rusting of iron cramps. For this reason the whole of the parapets of the north porch had to be taken down in 1990 and renewed. At the same time the very badly shattered medieval canopy work and later statuary over the entrance arch was taken down, carefully replaced after removing the iron, and treated with a shelter coat (fig. 90). Also for public safety the pinnacle of the north west turret had to be taken down and rebuilt.

Rusting of the ironwork in the Tower pinnacles started to lift the masonry and cause severe fracturing and as a matter of urgency a major programme dismantling these features, removing the iron and rebuilding using the major part of the original stone was put in hand.

Where possible the upper parts of the pinnacles which appeared to be sound were left suspended off the scaffolding while the lower sections were removed. This work called for considerable skill and a high standard of craftmanship. Constant falls of render from the west face of the south west transept and heavy thermal scale on the masonry here together with very poor pointing and scaling on the east face led next to the setting up of a programme for work in this area (figs. 93 and 115). Advantage was taken of the necessary scaffolding for the masonry work to strip and recover the roof where some of the timber work was propped off the main vault. Appreciable masonry renewal was necessary on the centre point of the west face for structural reasons but the badly eroded area at the northern section of the wall was left untouched.

In 1992 a further programme of work was put in hand to strip and recover the nave roof and to utilise the scaffolding for the repair and replacement of defective masonry to the two nave clerestories and the south west pinnacle. Appreciable timber repairs had to be faced where the ends of trusses were built solidly into the clerestory walls and the structure of the roof was strengthened by the insertion of new metal cross ties. While the roof timbers were exposed the opportunity was taken to carry out a thorough historical investigation and to date some of the more important timbers by tree-ring dating. The results of this work are awaited (1994). Similar work will also have to be undertaken in due course to the eastern high roofs and all the lead lower roofs, with the exception of the two Nave aisles, will have to be replaced. In addition, major stone repairs are required round the whole Cathedral.

# 11. THE BUILDING STONES USED IN THE CATHEDRAL

BY PROFESSOR JOHN PRENTICE

In the middle of the wide alluvial plain of the Severn, there was no conveniently close source of stone for the builders of the Cathedral. At the same time, they turned proximity to the river to advantage, and sought their stone where the river allowed easy transport of the huge amounts of rock from quarry to Cathedral. Many different stones have gone to build the edifice we see today.

*Highley Stone,* of Carboniferous age, comes from the higher reaches of the Severn between Kidderminster and Bridgnorth, some 35 kilometres above Worcester; the huge riverside quarries can still be seen today. It is a uniformly greenish-grey sandstone, sparsely speckled with mica, and with white spots indicating the presence of feldspar.

Just across the river from Highley village, the quarries provided *Alveley Stone*, a sandstone a little younger in Carboniferous age. Also greyish-green in colour, it is conspicuously mottled with irregular patches of dark reddish or purplish brown.

Much nearer to Worcester, but still accessible to the river, a group of quarries at Holt, Ombersley and Hadley, produced *Holt Stone*, an Upper Triassic sandstone. Superficially similar to Alveley Stone, it is a lighter grey colour, and the mottling is red rather than brown. It is also very much softer.

In the Cathedral structure, from its earliest stages, there is much use of Jurassic Öolitic Limestone. Many different types can be identified, pointing to a number of different sources in the Cotswold Hills. Since Roman times these limestones have been much appreciated as building stones, and quarries at Cutsdean, Daglingworth and Guiting, known to have had a long history, could have been the sources - but all involve long overland haulage. The source of some could be Hawkesbury, south of Wotton-under-Edge, where the abbey is known to have had quarries, and which is not too distant from the Severn estuary.

The stone which is conspicuous by its absence, however, is the Blue Lias Limestone. The nearest hard rock, with many quarries in the vales of Evesham and Severn, and used extensively in humbler buildings of the same date, and in walls around the precinct itself, it finds little place in the grander Cathedral structure.

The rock which, in the geological sense, is the youngest is Tufa. This calcareous rock is deposited by lime-rich springs and streams, and is found in many scattered localities in Herefordshire. It is white or cream in colour, and contains abundant casts of plant stems – this gives it a conspicuously porous texture and makes the rock extremely light in weight.

The pre-Conquest fabric in the West Cloister is of Alveley Stone; but the Saxon pillars in the east slype are of an öolitic limestone tentatively identified as from Guiting. The 11th century pillars of the crypt are also of Jurassic limestone, but of a different type. It is interesting to note the ingenuity with which the builders used this obviously scarce material - some pillars are intact blocks placed vertically, others made up of small pieces - and one pillar is Highley Stone.

The use of alternate bands of pale Öolitic Limestone with dark Highley Stone is seen in the Chapter House, in the early 12th century pillars of the Nave, and in the Tower staircases. In contrast the later 12th century work, well seen at the western exterior of the Nave and north aisle, was almost entirely in Highley Stone. This seems to have continued into the 13th century on the exterior, but the interior work of this date is largely of Cotswold Öolite.

A conspicuous feature of the 13th century Choir and Lady Chapel is the use of Purbeck 'Marble'. This is a dark-grey fossiliferous limestone, quarried intensively on the coast of Dorset. The alternation of pillars of this with the light coloured Öolitic Limestone in the main arcades is most striking. Some of these pillars cannot be positively identified as Purbeck 'marble' - there may be some use of local Liassic material here. Some earlier use of Purbeck stone can be found in the colonettes of the small doorway leading into College Green from the passage below College Hall, whose Romanesque form suggests a 12th century date; and in the effigy and chest of King John's tomb. The slab below this effigy is, however, another imported stone, the *mabre noir de Dinant* - a Devonian limestone from Belgium much used in English Abbeys of that time. More recent use of the latter is seen in the steps leading upwards on either side of the Choir

The 14th century vaulting of the Nave contains a variety of stone, but at the western end there are substantial areas of Tufa. It has been suggested that these are re-used from an earlier vault entirely made up of this. Because of its lightness, Tufa has always been valued as a roofing stone, but it has always been in short supply.

The 14th and 15th century building saw the introduction of Holt Stone, with Alveley Stone used for bases and buttresses. The use of Holt Stone, which weathers very readily, for much of the exterior has occasioned a process of replacement which continues until the present day. Until 1870 the replacement stone was Holt Stone, but with the closure of the quarry, other Triassic sandstones, notably from Grinshill in Shropshire, and Hollington in Staffordshire, have been used, as well as some imported from Germany. The result is a patchwork which gives Worcester Cathedral the unique appearance it has today.

# GLOSSARY

ABACUS: the flat slab on the top of a capital (*q.v.*)

AMBULATORY:  semicircular or polygonal aisle enclosing an apse (*q.v.*)

APSE: vaulted semicircular or polygonal end of a chancel or a chapel.

ARCADE: range of arches supported on free-standing piers or columns; BLIND ARCADE, the same attached to a wall

ASHLAR: masonry of large squared blocks

BAYS: internal compartments of a building

BLOCK CAPITAL: Romanesque capital cut from a cube by having the lower angles rounded off to a circular shaft below (also called Cushion Capital)

CANOPY: projection or hood over an altar, pulpit, niche, statue, etc.

CAPITAL: the top part of a column, usually decorative

CHANCEL: the whole of the church  east of the crossing excluding the Lady Chapel

CHANTRY CHAPEL: chapel attached to, or inside, a church endowed for the saying  of Masses for the soul of the founder

CHAMFER: surface made by  cutting the square edge of a block at an angle of 45°

CHEVRON: Norman moulding forming a zig-zag

CHOIR  (QUIRE): that part of the church where divine service is sung

CLERESTORY: upper storey of the nave walls of a church, pierced by windows

CRENELLATION: parapet with a series of embrasures with  raised portions or merlons between

CROCKET, CROCKETING: decorative features placed on the sloping sides of spires pinnacles, gables, etc. in Gothic architecture, carved in various leaf shapes and placed at regular intervals

CROCKET CAPITAL: An early Gothic form of stylised leaf shapes

CROSSING: the intersection of the nave, chancel and transepts

CRYPT: underground room usually below the east  end of the church

CUSHION CAPITAL: see Block Capital

CUSP: projecting point between small arcs in Gothic tracery.

DECORATED: style of English Gothic architecture from c.1250 to c.1350.

DOGTOOTH: typical E.E. ornament consisting of four-cornered stars raised pyramidally.

EARLY ENGLISH (E.E.): historical division of English Gothic architecture roughly covering the 13th century

EMBRASURES:  regular openings in a parapet

ENGAGED COLUMNS: columns attached to, or partly sunk into, a wall

FILLET: narrow flat band running down a shaft or along a roll moulding (*q.v.*)

FINIAL: top of a canopy, gable, or pinnacle

GALLERY: in church architecture the upper storey above an aisle, opening in arches to the nave.   Also called Tribune but often erroneously Triforium (*q.v.*)

GROIN: sharp edge at the meeting of a cross-vault.  Sometimes called an ARRIS

IMPOST: bracket in a wall, usually formed of mouldings, on which the ends of an arch rest

JAMB: straight side of an archway, doorway, or window

LANCET WINDOW: slender pointed-arched window

LANTERN: in architecture, a turret with windows all round crowning a roof or a dome

LIERNE: see Vault

MISERICORD: bracket on the underside of a hinged choir stall seat which, when lifted up, gave the occupant of the seat a support during long periods of standing (also called Miserere)

NAIL-HEAD: E.E. ornamental motif, consisting of regularly repeated small pyramids

PATERA: small flat circular or oval ornament

PENDANT: boss elongated so that it seems to hang down

PERPENDICULAR: style of English Gothic architecture covering the period from c.1335-50 to c.1530

PIER: strong, solid support, frequently square in section or of composite section (compound pier)

PILASTER: shallow pier attached to a wall

PINNACLE: ornamental form crowning a spire, tower, buttress, etc.,

PLINTH: projecting base of a wall or column, generally chamfered (q.v.) or moulded at the top

PRESBYTERY: the part of the church lying E of the choir containing the altar

PULPITUM: stone screen in a major church provided to shut off the choir from the nave

QUOINS: dressed stones at the angles of a building. Often they are alternately large and small

RADIATING CHAPELS: chapels projecting radially from an ambulatory or an apse

REFECTORY: dining hall

REREDOS: structure behind and above an altar

RESPOND: half-pier bonded into a wall and carrying one end of an arch

ROLL-MOULDING: moulding of semicircular or more than semicircular section

ROMANESQUE: style in architecture which was current in the 11th and 12th centuries and preceded the Gothic style (in England often called Norman)

ROOD: cross or crucifix

SANCTUARY: area around the main altar of a church

SCREEN: Parclose screen: screen separating a chapel from the rest of a church. Rood screen: screen below the rood, usually at the west end of a chancel

SEDILIA: seats for the priests (usually three) on the south side of the chancel of a church

SHAFT-RING: 12th and 13th centuries feature consisting of a ring round a circular pier or a shaft attached to a pier

SOFFIT: underside of an arch, lintel, etc

SLYPE: A passage, usually in the form of a tunnel, leading from the Cloisters to the precinct. The Eastern Slype led to the Monks' cemetery

SPANDREL: triangular surface between two arches

SPLAY: chamfer, usually of the jamb of a window

STALL: carved seat made of wood or stone

STIFF-LEAF: E.E. type of foliage of many-lobed shapes

STOUP: vessel for holding of holy water, usually placed near a door

STRING COURSE: projecting horizontal band or moulding set in the surface of a wall

TIERCERON: see Vault

TRACERY: ribwork in the upper part of a window, or used decoratively in blank arches on vaults

TRANSEPT: transverse part of a cross-shaped church

TREFOIL, QUATREFOIL or CINQUEFOIL: three, four or five lobes or leaf shapes in Gothic tracery

TRIBUNE: see Gallery

TRIFORIUM, TRIFORIA: arcaded wall passage or blank arcading facing the nave at the height of the aisle roof and below the clerestory (*q.v.*) windows (see Gallery.)

TYMPANUM: space between the lintel of a doorway and the arch above it

VAULT: *Barrel vault, tunnel vault*: vault of semi-circular section; *Groin vault*: identical shapes intersecting each other, as in the Worcester Crypt; *Lierne*: tertiary rib, that is a rib which does not spring either from one of the main springers or from the central boss. (see figs. 84, 85 and 87 ); *Ribbed vault*: vault with ribs added to the groins (see fig. 62); *Ridge rib*: rib along the longitudinal or transverse ridge of the vault-early 13th century; *Tierceron*; secondary rib, a rib which issues from the springing of the vault or the central boss and leads to place on the ridge rib (see fig. 72)

VOUSSOIR: wedge-shaped stone used in arch construction

WATERLEAF: leaf shape used in later 12th century capitals

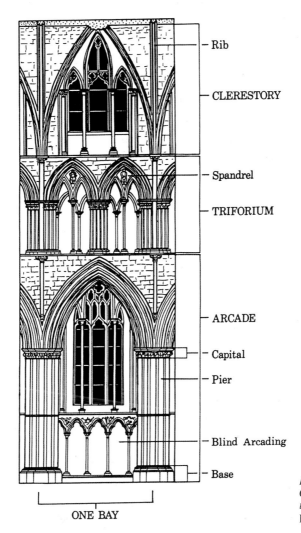

— Rib

— CLERESTORY

— Spandrel

— TRIFORIUM

— ARCADE

— Capital

— Pier

— Blind Arcading

— Base

ONE BAY

*Fig 120. One bay of the Choir showing the terms used to describe its parts.* Drawn by Helen Lubin.

# BIBLIOGRAPHY

There is a dearth of accessible publications on the architecture, sculpture, painting and stained glass of the Cathedral and it is hoped that this book will be the first of a series which will cover every aspect of the Cathedral's development.

The most important sources for this book have been the papers by the Rev Robert Willis, dating from the mid-nineteenth century but even now only superseded in detail; the entry for the Cathedral in Pevsner's *Worcestershire*, and the papers resulting from the visit of the British Archaeological Association in 1975.

Baker, N. *et al.* From Roman to Medieval Worcester : development and planning in the Anglo-Saxon City, *Antiquity*, Vol. 66, No. 250, March 1992, 65-74

Barker, P.A. ed. *The Origins of Worcester; Trans. Worcs. Archaeol. Soc.* 3rd series, Vol. 2 1968-69  Worcester 1970, (particularly pp. 27-34)

Barker, P.A., Cubberley, A.L., Crowfoot, E. and Radford, C.A.R. Two burials under the Refectory at Worcester Cathedral, *Med.Archaeol.* 18 (1974), 146-151

Bassett, S. Churches in Worcester before and after the conversion of the Anglo-Saxons, *The Antiquaries Journal*, Vol LXIX, Part II, 1989 pp. 225-256

Carver, M.O.H. ed. *Medieval Worcester: An Archaeological Framework; Trans. Worcs. Archaeol. Soc.* 3rd series, Vol 7 1980. (particularly pp. 31ff, 115ff, 127ff, 139ff, 143ff, and 298-300.)

Craze, M. *Lectures on Worcester Cathedral*, Worcester 1988

Guy, C. Forthcoming, 1994-95, *Worcs. Archaeol. Soc. Trans.* Vol. 14

Henry, Avril, ed. *The Eton Roundels, Eton College, Ms 177*, Scolar Press, 1991

Lubin, H. *The Worcester Pilgrim*, Worcester, 1990. Describes the discovery of a well-preserved Pilgrim burial in the Crossing of the Cathedral, and discusses its implications.

*Medieval Art and Architecture at Worcester Cathedral, British Archaeological Association Transactions for the year 1975*, London, 1978. Includes an extensive bibliography relating to the Cathedral.

Pevsner, N. *The Buildings of England: Worcestershire* Penguin, 1968, pp 293-314

Willis Bund, J.W. *The Civil War in Worcestershire 1643-1646* and *The Scotch Invasion of 1651*, Birmingham 1905

*Worcester Cathedral Notes and Monographs 1909-1914*, Cathedral Library. A miscellany of important papers relating to the architecture and sculpture of the Cathedral.

Wild, C. *An illustration of the Architecture and Sculpture of the Cathedral Church of Worcester*, London, 1823

Willis, R. The Architectural History of the Cathedral and Monastery at Worcester, *Archaeol . Journ.*, XX (1863), pp 83, 254, 301

Willis, R. The Crypt and the Chapter House of Worcester Cathedral, *RIBA Journal* XIII (1862/ 63), p 213

Willis, R. Notes on the Norman Work in the Chapter House of Worcester Cathedral, *Archaeol Journ.*, XX (1863), p.17

The Reports of the Symposia on the Precinct of the Cathedral at Worcester 1991, 1992, 1993. Worcester Chapter Office

# ACKNOWLEDGEMENTS

Thanks are due to all the following for their indispensible help in the production of this book:

The Dean and Chapter of Worcester and Captain Colin Wilson, the Chapter Clerk.

Canon Iain MacKenzie, the Cathedral Librarian, and his staff, for help with the documentary evidence.

Mr Kenneth Wiltshire, the Cathedral Architect, for discussions on the problems of the structure and in particular for Chapter 10.

Posthumously, alas, the former Cathedral Architect, Mr Bernard Ashwell, for his enthusiastic discussions on the building and its archaeological problems.

Mr Brian Eacock, the Clerk of Works, and his staff for discussions on every aspect of the Cathedral fabric.

The Vergers, for their tolerance.

Dr. Richard Gem, Secretary of the Cathedrals Fabric Commission, for his advice, particularly on the Norman Cathedral.

Dr. Richard Lockett for help with Chapter 9, the 19th century Restoration.

Drs. Nigel Baker and Richard Holt, and Mr Hal Dalwood for help with Chapter 2.

Professor John Prentice for the section on the stones used in the Cathedral.

Mr Chris Guy, the Cathedral Archaeologist, for ongoing help and discussion.

Miss Helen Lubin, the former Cathedral Archaeologist, for her help and discussion during her work here.

Sidney Renow, for photographic processing of a high order.

Stratascan for figure 93.

Mrs Lynne MacKenzie for her help with the excavations.

And not least, Mrs Christine Priddey for her patience in word-processing the evolving manuscript.

The photographs are by the author except where otherwise attributed